The Pornography
of Meat

The Pornography of Meat

CAROL J. ADAMS

⚡ **continuum**
NEW YORK • LONDON

2003

The Continuum International Publishing Group Inc
370 Lexington Avenue, New York, NY 10017

The Continuum International Publishing Group Ltd
The Tower Building, 11 York Road, London SE1 7NX

Printed in the United States of America

Text design by Susan Mark Huie

Library of Congress Cataloging-in-Publication Data

Adams, Carol J.
   The pornography of meat / Carol J. Adams.
      p. cm.
   ISBN 0-8264-1448-6
   1. Body, Human—Social aspects.   2. Body image.   3. Women in
   popular culture.   4. Pornography.   5. Vegetarianism.   I. Title
   HM636.A33 2003
   306.4—dc21   2002155480

For Marie M. Fortune and Mary E. Hunt
*"I never grew discouraged because I knew that
my cause was just, and I was always in good company."*

—SUSAN B. ANTHONY

Contents

1   What Pornography?   11

2   More than Meat   19

3   Man to Man   27

4   Yoked Oppressions   39

5   Beasts   49

6   Hamtastic   61

7   Body Chopping   73

8   Armed Hunters   83

9   Hookers   97

10 The Fish in Water Problem   103

11 Anthropornography   109

12 I Ate a Pig   117

13 Average White Girl   127

14 Hoofing It   135

15 The Female of the Species   147

16 Male Chauvinist Pig?   159

    Epilogue   179

    Acknowledgments   181

    Citations   188

Meat is like pornography:
before it was someone's fun,
it was someone's life.

—MELINDA VADAS

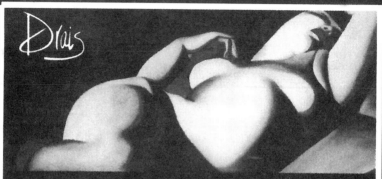

1

What Pornography?

EVERYWHERE we turn, consuming images—and more—are in our face.

In Germany, some restaurants served sushi and raw fish on top of a naked woman who was lying spread-eagled on her back.

In France, *maison's d'abattage* ("houses of slaughter") involve the prostitution of young women—six or seven girls each serving 80 to 120 customers a night.

In the United States, a *Cosby* television show episode included the son Theo and his friend referring to women as "burgers," "double burgers," and "deluxe burgers."

A young prostitute is known as *fresh meat*; an older prostitute, *dead meat*. At one point, *mutton* meant prostitute, as in Shakespeare's reference in *Measure for Measure*: "The duke . . . would eat mutton on Fridays." *Mutton dressed as a lamb* is a derogatory comment about a woman who is attempting to dress and appear younger than she is.

An episode of the television show *China Beach* that featured the murder of a prostitute ended with a monologue about working in a meat-packing plant.

In California, a supermarket butcher was fired from his job for intentionally cutting meat to resemble female genitalia.

An episode of *Fresh Prince* featured the character Will saying to the character Carleton about the women at a nearby club: "There's some 100% USDA Prime Choice down there. I could be tenderizing some right now."

In the sixteenth century, a madrigal called "The Big Fat Goose," full of double entendres, tells the story of a farmer "who had a big fat goose / a dandy goose" with "a nice long, big, fat, juicy, tender curving neck." The song continues:

> *Bring on this goose,*
> *Let us put her to use!*
> *Pluck her, stuff her, broil her, roast her, carve her, eat her!*

In the twenty-first century, a Thanksgiving message circulated on the Internet that describes a man laying "her" on the table, rubbing her, touching her neck, breast, and thigh, his arousal is tracked from sweating to drooling to a joyous cry when he touches

> *the hole . . . dark and murky*
> *He rubbed his hands and licked his lips. . . .*
> *And then he stuffed the turkey.*

WE
SERVE
THE
BEST
MEAT
IN
TOWN

THE HUSTLER®
9th & Vincent · Cleveland

One *Penthouse* cartoon showed a kneeling, bare-chested man with his hands folded together in front of him in prayer, saying ". . . and for what we are about to receive we are truly thankful. . . ." He is at the side of his bed, and on the bed is a turkey—a dead, beheaded turkey dressed in a bra, garters, and stockings.

Viewing other beings as consumable is a central aspect of our culture.

The New Yorker's Terrence Rafferty called *Hustler* magazine, "meat-and-potatoes sex for the working man (or, more precisely, just meat)." Originally, *Hustler* was a purveyor of "meat" (as in dead animals) at a club with this image on the back of the menu. But Larry Flynt figured out where the real money is. (Being an unregulated market, it is hard to estimate profits from pornography. But in 1998, the profits were thought to be between $10 and $20 billion.)

Pornographers know what sells. Like a restaurant that transforms itself into a pornographic magazine, advertisers want "in" to this amazingly successful media.

Live. Nude. Lobsters. What other kinds are there?

Pleasurable consumption of consumable beings is the dominant perspective of our culture. It is what subjects do to objects, what someone does with something.

And so the question that comes to mind is just how does some*one* become some*thing*? How *does* someone come to be viewed as an object, a product, as consumable? How does her use to another as this product, this consumable object, become more important than her own inherent value, her own complete and unique self?

The question, truly, is how does someone become a piece of meat?

And the answer is, we really don't want to know.

In July, 2002, a woman looked from her third-floor apartment in Liberty, Missouri, and saw a group of people, standing around a barbeque grill. Asked what they were cooking, they told her "pussy." Asked again, they said "pussy" again, and added some cat noises. When she prodded further, one of

the men responded, "Want to see if your fat ass can save it?" At this, the woman rushed down the stairs, and grabbed a kitten out from the coals.

Before someone can be consumed or used, she has to be seen as consumable, as usable, as a some*thing* instead of a some*one*. This process of viewing another as consumable—as something—is usually invisible to us. Its invisibility occurs because it corresponds to the view of the dominant culture.

The process is also invisible because the end product of the process—the object of consumption—is available everywhere. We don't realize that the act of *viewing* another as an object and the act of *believing* that another is an object are actually different acts, because our culture has collapsed them into one.

Advertisements are never only about the product they are promoting. They are about how our culture is structured, what we believe about ourselves and others. Advertisements appeal to *someone* to buy *something*. In this, they offer a window into the myths by which our world is structured—who are the some-ones in our culture, and who become the somethings?

Reporter F. K. Plous offers one answer to that question. Plous frequented a Chicago store owned by Bob Miller that kills its chickens in-

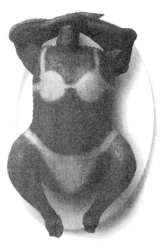

Chicken never looked so good in a microwave.

LG's InHelp COVER not only cooks fast and evenly, but it also browns and grills like a conventional oven. This stylish stainless steel model is part of LG's great selection of microwaves. Sizes range from the 30L microwave to the 42L family-sized model. And they all come with our exclusive 2–3 year warranty. **Life's Good** LG

When alive, crowded together in factory farms, a "broiler" chicken at maturity has an average of half of a square foot of space in which to live. In that microwave, the chicken had more room than she ever did when alive.

dividually for each customer. Plous not only wanted to watch the process, he wanted to kill his own chicken.

Miller told Plous to hold the chicken's wings, and with the same hand, pull the head back. With the other hand, he used a straight razor, pressing it against the chicken's gullet. After the chicken's throat was cut, she was stuffed head-down into a "funnel," and the blood drained away. When the blood stopped flowing, the chicken was immersed in a scalding tank. After 40 seconds, the chicken was removed and carried to the plucking machine. Plous tells us what he saw at this point:

A dead and scalded chicken is both an appalling and a hilarious sight. Most surprising of all is its true size: skinny, absurdly skinny, a characteristic withheld from patrons of supermarkets, where the chickens are sold sans feet, their necks jammed inside the body cavity and their scrawny carcasses squeezed into spurious plumpness by tight fitting paper tubs tightened even further by tough plastic wrappers.

Perhaps Plous is thinking along lines such as the above photo: Chicken parts packaged as though by the designer Calvin Klein: "Great Legs. Nice Breasts."

Of the dead and scalded chicken before him, Plous remarks:

Miller's back room employs no such cosmetics [as plastic wrappers and tight fitting tubs], and for the chicken lover the result is an appalling and funny overdose of truth, sort of like a centerfold feature showing the Playmate of the Month undergoing a gynecological exam.

Plous is not alone in being a pornography user. *Listening to Prozac* opens with the story of how the author, Peter Kramer, prescribed Prozac to his patient Sam, who was suffering from melancholy. According to Kramer, "Sam not only recovered from his depression, he declared himself 'better than well.'"

One detail of this cure troubled Sam. He had previously prided himself on his "independent" style in sexual matters. Kramer explains, "A central conflict in his marriage was his interest in pornographic videos. He insisted his wife watch hard-core films with him despite her distaste." Once Sam was on Prozac he enjoyed sex as much as ever but he lost interest in pornography. This bothered Sam: "something that had seemed essential about his personality" had been redefined.

Both Kramer the therapist and the many reviewers of his books, including ones who offered this example from it, accepted the fact that "Sam" forcing his partner to use pornography was his right and privilege, essential to his sense of self, his "independent style." Kramer acknowledges in his next sentence that "shortly after Sam reported his loss of interest in pornography," he, Kramer, made two ordinary mistakes. But he never seemed to notice that he had already made one significant mistake.

Why was Sam's use of pornography and coercion of his wife unremarked upon? Did Kramer ever think to wonder what Sam's wife thought about the "cure"? Perhaps she was delighted by the results of his therapy. One hopes it brought her relief from sexual activity to which she may have submitted but did not consent.

For Sam, like most users of pornography, looking at pornography is repetitive behavior, cued to arousal.

In the following pages we will see how pornographic photographs, like advertisements, are carefully constructed: nothing that appears in the photograph or the advertisement is there by accident. What is placed in photo-

graphs sends cues to users. Users like Sam learn to be sexually receptive to the cues built into pornography.

Some readers may feel aroused when encountering in these pages the pornographic positioning of women and nonhuman animals; others, like Sam's wife, will feel distaste.

Analyzing the pornographic cues helps to remove their power but also exposes those of us not so cued to a hostile worldview. Some of the images are upsetting. You, the reader, should give yourself permission to respond to what you encounter. Ask yourself, "What am I going through?" "What am I feeling?"

The rooster is asking, "What pornography?"

I have written this book and included these disturbing images because we cannot challenge or change what we do not comprehend.

Inequality is clearly a part of our relationships with the other animals, otherwise we could not experiment upon them, display, hunt, kill, and eat them. The presence of animals in pornography and advertisements is a reminder of a basic inequality—but whose?

Into the void of a no-state-regulation Russia after the demise of the Soviet Union came a wave of pornography and prostitution. Businesses appeared whose only purpose was to market Russian women to the West as prostitutes, strippers, and mail-order brides. In 1992, Fred Weir reported in the *Guardian* about the "unease" that was growing across the political spectrum in Russia in response to the rise in what he called the "sex-for-sale" business (actually, as his article shows, it was "woman-for-sale" businesses).

"What pornography?" appeared around this time in a Russian business magazine. It depicts inequality: one being is alive and whole, the other being is dead and scalded. Clearly, someone consumes something, and that someone is male.

What pornography?

This pornography: the pornography of meat.

2

More than Meat

MORE THAN MEAT

WE ARE EACH MORE THAN MEAT, more than our bodies. Yes, in some sense we are made up of meat, of muscle. But we would never want to be seen only as meat.

"Don't treat me like a piece of meat!" What does that cry say except, "I am more than meat! I am not something! I have feelings!"

Still, that cry is a reminder that someone else *is* a piece of meat, that someone else has been violently separated from her or his body; that a consumer has become the consumed; that a subject is now an object.

How did we come to accept that animals are destined to be no more than meat?

When you were growing up, your children's section of the local newspaper might have told you "All about Sheep." It explained: *Sheep furnish us wool. Sheep furnish us food. Sheep furnish us milk. Sheep furnish us leather.*

It sounds so innocuous doesn't it? Just how do those sheep furnish us food? Perhaps you thought they died of old age, as one child believed: "But when I was eight I found out that wasn't true—that animals were killed! I ran home for reassurance. *We didn't eat meat like that, did we?*"

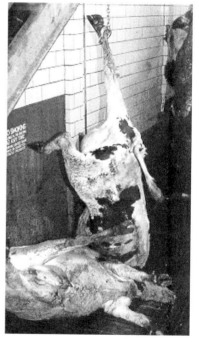

Perhaps like Calvin you might have wondered where hamburger meat came from.

And when you realized it was from cows, perhaps you protested that you couldn't finish your meal. Then you might have been told:

"*The cows don't suffer.*"

"*The cow* wanted *to be your food.*"

"*You need to eat meat or else you will die.*"

"*If you want your dessert, you have to finish your hamburger.*"

"*That is why cows exist.*"

You took the fact that you were eating a cow and had to swallow that as well as the hamburger.

I know I did. I did and I knew what butchering was. When I was a child, I had watched the local butcher kill, disembowel, skin, and slice up cows and pigs.

Sandra Bartky observes that feminists don't see different things from other people, they see the same thing differently. When I was 21, after my first year

MARIE FORTUNE

at Yale University Divinity School, I returned to my hometown in western New York. As I was unpacking, I heard a knock at the door. It was an urgent, insistent knock. I ran downstairs, and a neighbor shouted to me, "someone has just shot your horse!" Following him, we rushed to the pasture and there was Jimmy, our aged pony, lying dead. In the distance, we could hear shots.

That night at supper, I bit into a hamburger.

Suddenly that hamburger was larger than life. I flashed on the image of Jimmy's dead body waiting to be buried in the morning. I thought: "I am eating a dead cow."

Like Lisa Simpson, I, too, knew what it was like to look at a nonhuman animal and have an individual look back at me—not as a (human) subject gazing at an (animal) object, but as two subjects. After that experience at dinner, I saw the same thing differently.

no longer now
He slays the lamb that
looks him in the face,
And horribly devours his
mangled flesh (viii. 211)
—Percy Shelley, *Queen Mab*

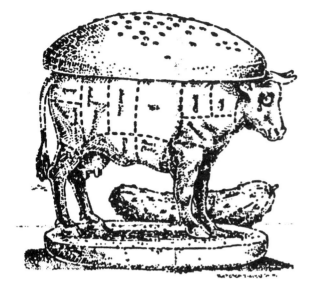

When a hamburger is eaten, no one looks harmed. But that is because someone, a unique being, has become something, an object, with no distinctiveness, no uniqueness, no individuality. Someone has become a *mass term*.

Mass terms refer to things like water or colors; no matter how much you have of it, or what type of container it is in, it remains the same: water remains water; red stays red. You can add a bucket of water to a pool of water without changing "water"; you can mix red with red and you still have "red."

When you add five pounds of hamburger to a plate of hamburger, it is more of the same thing, nothing is changed. But if you have a living cow in front of you, and you kill that cow, and

FARM

butcher that cow, and grind up her body, you have not added a mass term to a mass term and ended up with more of the same.

What is on the plate in front of us is not devoid of specificity; it is the dead flesh of what was once a living, feeling being.

The crucial point here is that we make someone who is a unique being into something that is the appropriate referent of a mass term.

Mass terms signal the *thingification* of beings.

In the summer of 2000, New York City hosted more than 500 life-sized fiberglass cows that had been decorated by artists. They were placed around the five boroughs of New York in a so-called CowParade. Among fanciful and colorful cows like a Rockette cow, a surfing cow, and a taxi cow, was filmmaker David Lynch's *Eat My Fear* cow.

This cow had not "died" of old age. With forks and knives stuck into the cow's behind, the bloody disemboweled cow was displayed for only a couple of hours. During that time, according to *New Yorker* writer Tad Friend, at least one small child, upon seeing it, started crying. Then it was banished to a warehouse and put under wraps.

Why was this cow banned from the CowParade? We do not want to experience uncomfortable feelings about violence, butchering, suffering, and fear. This is the function of the *absent referent*—to keep our "meat" separated from any idea that she or he was once an animal who was butchered, to keep some*thing* (like hamburger) from being seen as having been some-*one* (a cow, a lamb, a once-alive being, a subject.)

With the absent referent, we do not have to ask of someone, "What are you going through?" since there is no one there to ask.

Formula for the absent referent
nonhuman animal + butchering =
"meat"/consumable flesh/mass term

Whereas meat eating requires violence, the absent referent functions to put the violence under wraps: there is no "cow" whom we have to think about, there is no butchering, no feelings, and no fear, just the end product. (And David Lynch is correct: people eat animals' fear. Nonhumans who experience fear before death release adrenalin that can leave soft, mushy spots in their "meat," making their flesh tougher.)

With the absent referent, we do not have to see meat eating as contact with a once-living individual because it has been renamed as contact with *food*. We do not have to think, "I am now interacting with a unique being, someone whom I required be violently killed and dismembered."

We will no longer hang women up like pieces of meat.
–Larry Flynt

CAROL J. ADAMS INTERPRETING IMAGE AT HER SLIDE SHOW.
PHOTO BY JUAN GARCIA

This cover shows precisely how butchering works to convert someone into something. Someone with a very specific life becomes part of a mass term, interchangeable hamburger meat.

Using a woman reveals how this ordinary act of violence—grinding up a nonhuman body—can be seen as an extreme violation when it is depicted as happening to someone who matters, or seems to matter. The resonance of familiarity with this human body heightens awareness of the violence. Yet, one of the purposes of pornography is to establish women's differences from men.

There is familiarity in the human leg, but there is difference, too—this human leg is shaved, and glistens with grease. It is marked as female. Larry Flynt's assurance that "women" will not be hung up like pieces of meat reminds us that of course women will be. Women, not men.

Although butchering makes someone into something, the *Hustler* cover illustrates more: someone *already* had become something for this image to be created, someone had become a sexually marked body . . . a human female body.

Pornography uses butchery to say something about women's status as mass terms: women are as meat; not only that, women deserve to be treated as meat—butchered and consumed. Of course laws prevent butchering human beings. (Not that this has kept some people, predominantly men, from butchering their sexual partners, predominantly women.)

With pornography, fragmented body parts become sexualized so that someone can get pleasure from something. Yet that *something*—the woman used in pornography—was at one point someone, a very specific someone. Two mass terms are merged as one—individual animals into hamburger, an individual woman into an object "woman." Through this doubling of objectification, what we have before us is the butchering of women's subject status.

Formula for the absent referent
nonhuman/or human substitute + butchering =
"meat"/consumable flesh/mass term/
destruction of subject status

Are we each really more than meat? Or are women, like the other animals, *less* more than meat than men?

Note the reference to "Pick-up" only.
And printed on recycled paper—how reassuring!

3

Man to Man

IN 1959, VICE PRESIDENT Richard Nixon visited Moscow and met with Soviet Secretary Nikita Krushchev. As the two leaders toured an exhibit of a model American home, Nixon suddenly poked Krushchev in the chest.

What did Nixon say to Krushchev in the infamous "kitchen debates"? According to Elliott Erwitt, the photographer who captured the picture of Nixon's violent jab, Nixon said: "We, in America, eat a lot more meat than you do. You eat a lot more cabbage." Translation: America can beat you vegetable-eaters any day!

What was Krushchev's response?

ELLIOTT ERWITT/MAGNUM PHOTOS

He said, "You can [expletive] my grandmother."

Almost thirty years later, Boris Yeltsin, then President of Russia, deflecting an attempt by then-Secretary of State Warren Christopher to discuss barriers to trade in chicken parts, responded by saying, "Presidents don't do chicken legs. If, however, they were women's legs. . . ."

Sexual humor about women's and nonhumans' bodies teaches men how to look at women and teaches women how to be looked at and used.

The owl's eyes in the Hooters's logo show not just *what* is to be seen (breasts) but also *how* to look (in a fragmenting, objectifying way) and who is looking (a subject is looking at an object). The Hooters's menu makes this clear:

Now the dilemma . . . what to name the place. Simple . . . what else brings a gleam to men's eyes everywhere besides beer and chicken wings and an occasional winning football season? Hence, the name—Hooters—it is supposed that they were into owls.

In men's clubs, where *everything* is mouthwatering, women's objectification is entertaining. Even without actual food, pornography provides this context, too. Not by serving food identified with men's appetites (chicken wings?), but by renaming women *Taffy, Candy, Cookie, tasty chick.*

Language about meat or about the other animals, e.g., "owls" can become the vernacular for public (that is, *male)* talk about women.

As Hooters tell us, this language must speak to men though appear to be speaking to anyone. It must be associated with "men's" interests, especially a winning football season. It must be sexual; slang is important, and double entrendres make it fun.

When it comes to restaurants and newspapers, it's just one big men's club. Popsy, in the Pizza Nova flier, is not alone in *talkin' chicks.*

"When I chase chickens they wear skirts!" exclaimed a character in the film *Blaze of Noon.*

A radio ad encouraged listeners to *visit Davies Ford and take a hot chick for a test drive and take her home with you . . . you can also attend the live peep show at either of the two Davies Ford locations.* A peep show, as Marc Santora of the *New York Times* reminds us, involves a live woman. After payment, "a visor lifts, revealing the girl. She strips, the visor goes down, the lights go on. Peep show over."

The "peep show" promoted by the Ford dealership involved giving away baby chicks. Because they weren't concerned about the fate of these individual real life chicks, their promotion was curtailed after complaints from local humane groups. Peep show over.

On July 2, 1999, the *Dallas Morning News* ran a restaurant review of Pollo Fiesta, a popular Mexican–carryout restaurant. (One cannot eat a quiet meal there: "the unrelenting sound of a large meat cleaver deftly reducing a cooked chicken into its parts underscores each serving.")

MARIKA HOLMGREN

A photograph of the large grill overwhelms the words in the review. Off to the left side of the grill, a smiling young woman stands, flipping the cleaved bodies. Directly above the young woman and the sizzling body parts, the headline promises:

POLLO FIESTA: GOOD PLACE TO PICK UP CHICKS.

"Chick" may be an endearment when used in direct address, when someone (female) talks to another someone (female)—"Hey, where will we chicks eat?" But "chick" as a category, as a label, contains them within a larger framework: they are the dinner.

The nationally syndicated "Rubes" cartoon once showed three chickens gathered around one defeathered chick, who is saying, "It was awful. . . . First all my feathers were plucked. Then I was dipped in a bowl of flour, eggs, and water . . . But the worst part was being sprinkled with eleven different herbs and spices."

The caption? AT THE BATTERED CHICK SUPPORT GROUP.

The front of a card from American Greetings, categorized as "Birthday masculine," depicts a baby chick walking on sand saying ". . . must get . . . water . . . so . . . thirsty . . . can't . . . go on . . . much longer . . . water. . . ."

The birthday greeting inside reads: I KNOW HOW MUCH YOU LIKE TO SEE A HOT CHICK ON THE BEACH. So does the *New York Times!*

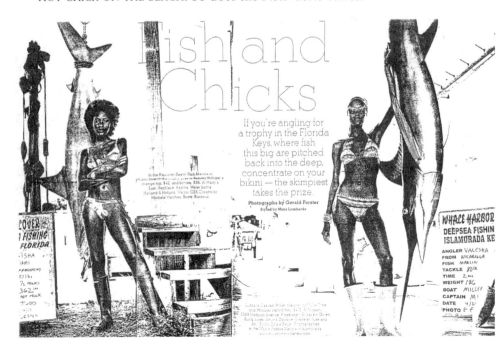

In a meat-eating culture, chicks exist to grow up and be eaten, which is why Pico can insist he is talkin' chicks when he referred to a "slow roasted 1/2 B.B.Q. [dead] chicken."

An attractive young woman is a *chicken dinner*. Racial adjectives further refine the term: "dark chicken meat" (in *Naked Lunch)* or "blond chicken" (in *In Cold Blood).*

Chicken also means *whore, prostitute.* A *chicken ranch* is a house of prostitution.

In the African American romantic comedy *Woo,* one character asks his girlfriend to dress up as a "chicken ho" because he loves fried chicken and "hos." He dresses up like a pimp, calling her a b****, and has her dress like a chicken, clucking and pecking at chickenfeed off his chest until she becomes disgusted and walks out.

A *chickenhawk* is a male who purchases either young men or young women. A *chicken queen* is a male who purchases young men.

Not a chickenhawk but a chicken farmer advises the most effective way to create emotional distance:

The first rule to remember if you plan on raising chickens for meat is never to name a bird you intend to eat! Either you won't be able to "do it" when the time comes, or that beautiful roast chicken will sit on the table while you and the kids sit around with tears in your eyes. If you must name your future meal, call it [sic] Colonel Sanders or Cacciatore.

As opposed to the upward ascent along what Arthur O. Lovejoy calls the Great Chain of Being, from nonhuman to human, exploitative language moves women and nonhumans down that Great Chain. Women are called by the names of other beings who are not free to determine their own identity, "pets," (sex) kitten, (Playboy) bunny, dog, beast, bird, bitch, heifer, sow, lamb, cow. Abusive epithets for young women have included hen, bird, flapper, quail, columbine, and, of course, chick—tasty or otherwise.

Exploitative language moves from the specific to the general: from the name of the individual to the name of a group of devalued individuals, *whores, chicks, bitches, bunnies, Cacciatore.* For instance, rapists and batterers instead of calling their victims by their given names, refer to them as *whore* or *cunt.* Renaming a "bird" you intend to beat or rape allows you to "do it" when the time comes.

Nonhumans move further down the vertical hierarchy, from live to dead

NANCY HILD, *CHICKEN, BITCH N' BUNNY*, 1990

object, becoming pieces of meat. Like the cleaver at Pollo Fiesta, exploitative language hacks the whole individual into a mass of attractive body parts. Women seen as "fuckable" are referred to as containers, holes, receptacles, as only body parts named *gash, slit, beaver, pussy, cunt, piece of ass.* Hooters's logo offers one answer to the old question posed by Colonel Sanders: "Are you a breast man or a leg man?"

Men talk about women—whether they know them or not—as sexually active *and* available to them: *a piece of ass* or a *whore.* Street sexual harassment includes words such as *broad, bitch, nooky, tail, tart.* Like *Cheep Date,* this language implies that every woman has a price.

Men with other men look and talk about women. Through rituals of dominance, they confirm their maleness to each other.

Let's take them at their literal word: these "men's clubs," these fraternities of "brothers," these "men's magazines" are teaching men and boys what it means to be men. And what does it take to be a man? Having sex with sexually objectified women.

Pornography is used by fraternities as education.

In *Ways of Seeing*, John Berger identifies how *Men look at women. Women watch themselves being looked at.* Gang rapes often take place within the environment of men's clubs committed by fraternity brothers and varsity athletes. Gang rape has also been called *spectoring,* confirming the important role of the male spectator to that event. There is also *voyeuring,* when one fraternity guy or jock has sex with a girl while others watch without her knowledge.

Man-to-man, women's status as sex object is the constant. Upon it, men write the story of their own subjectification. The sexual script is clear: men want sex; women are there to give sex or have it taken.

The language of the fraternity, and language of the pornographer, and language of the advertiser—all become one man-to-man language.

Psychotherapist Ellyn Kaschak proposes an alternative understanding to the oedipal complex in patriarchal societies. Through the education of men into male entitlement, men have extensive boundaries that engulf others, subsuming them, especially females, who are experienced as extensions of the man.

According to Kaschak, a man experiences himself as superior to women and as entitled to them. The man experiences sex as power, which can be manifested as sadism, violence or domination, which they name as "sex." Thus adult male sexuality becomes projected onto women, children, and the other animals.

Finally voyeurism, Kaschak points out, is an essential aspect of the construction of male psychology. The viewing and the believing become the same act; they become how they know that they each are someone—since they know that women and nonhumans are somethings.

By speaking the language of entitlement and by appealing to voyeuristic desires, meat advertisements are ways of affirming to men that they are a part of a larger group, a "fraternity" of men.

Hooters was not making a casual reference when it reminds us that "an occasional winning football season" also brings a gleam to men's eyes. Football is important to men because it seems to be an all-male pursuit; something that men can do, only men, not women. With its high male status, its almost total exclusion of women, and acceptable male violence, football allows for dominance bonding whether in steakhouses, in football stadiums, or at sports bars.

Linking meat eating with football and the male-sports culture is deliberate. College football players are often taken to steak houses the night before big games (and the amount of "steaks" each team eats is weighed, compared, and discussed in local papers).

According to Mariah Burton Nelson's *The Stronger Women Get the More Men Love Football*, a manly sports culture teaches men to love men and to hate women.

A manly sports culture teaches men to love steaks and to hate vegetarians.

The enormous growth of steakhouses in the past ten years, the success of chains like Morton's, the waiting lines of two hours on weekend nights in some cities . . . Why not read this phenomenon exactly as another headline in the *Dallas Morning News* did? as a "Male Call." The full headline for a review of "Bob's Steak and Chop House" that describes "how masculine" the environment is—a real "no-frills macho" place—declared: MALE CALL: BOB'S OUTPOST REPLICATES THE ORIGINAL'S MASCULINE, MEATY FORMULA.

Advertisements want each of us to see ourselves as unique individuals, the lone bull, not part of a herd, as "A Breed Apart" in the words of the Merrill Lynch ad that features a lone bull. Advertising promises individuality through the conformity of consumption.

A winning football season can't happen without a *football*.

And the football itself is summoned as another aspect of dominance, the "pigskin." No man is present in the "Home Sweet Home" cartoon, and yet the icon of the male sport's preserve, a football, reinforces the male point of view.

The pig is unperturbed by these parental images, enjoyably reading the daily newspaper, perhaps reading an ad for Johnsonville Brats that showed a hot dog in a bun shaped like a football and a real football, with the query SEPARATED AT BIRTH?

But to make sure we get the point, that this Home Sweet Home scene is

all OK, even with the orphaned pig, above the cartoon when it appeared in the *National Enquirer* was the statement, "Never cry over anything that can't cry over you."

Why must man-to-man language avoid tears?

Let's consider another aspect of this primal male act: the idea that eating meat, especially steaks, gives bull-length strength. Roger Porter's restaurant review *Prime Time* tells us, "I can think of no better place than Ruth's Chris Steak House to test your faith that the animal juice flowing into yours will restore your full-bloodedness and lend you a bull-like strength."

Henry David Thoreau pointed out 160 years ago that bulls get *their* strength from eating plant foods.

What is called "primal," "primitive" is shorthand for announcing a *male call*. It is here, in this environment, while eating big slabs of meat, that they are confirmed in their sense of identity. Vegetable protein doesn't bleed.

Meat eating becomes situated within two (albeit seemingly contradictory) givens—primal needs and triumphant, nonemotional rational morality.

This menu from the 1970s demonstrates the shaping of consumption patterns of those being trained to be dominant. Men are taught that they are beneficiaries of the system.

Note that the "Ladies' version" of the sirloin steak is *just as tasty*. . . .

And that the drink for women is "The Sissy." These convey the idea that men and women have different appetites. And then there is laughable Abigail Cathcart, from every menu peering out as a reminder of women's thwarted aspirations.

The more recent Frances Willard's matchbook is subtler. It helps if we know that she was president of the largest American women's organization of the nineteenth century, the Women's Christian Temperance Union. Not only that, she was a vegetarian. What sort of food and spirits are served over her dead body?

Poor Abigail Cathcart and Frances Willard—losers in a man's world. Both the menu and the matchbook cover implicitly remind men, "Our world is still secure. We won didn't we?"

Yet, there are some things man-to-man language fails to say. For instance, why *did* Americans eat more meat than the USSR in 1959? One reason is because in 1956, after successful lobbying by the meat and dairy industry, the USDA adopted the four-basic-foods pie chart. Fifty percent of the daily recommended food was now supposed to come from animal products.

And why wouldn't Russia relax the rules on importing chickens in 1996

THE VICTOR
BEAN & FEED
COMPANY
Eight Railroad Street · Victor, New York · 14564

MEET
ABIGAIL
CATHCART

An early advocate of womens' liberation, Miss Cathcart made an unsuccessful bid to become the first female bartender of the Bean & Feed.

MEN ENJOY THE FACT THAT WOMEN CAN'T GET ALL THE JOBS THAT MEN CAN.

when Yeltsin commented about women's legs to Christopher? Because dead chickens' parts from the United States were known to be dripping with salmonella.

And finally, what is ironic about the man-to-man language about eating meat? That a high-fat, meat-rich diet contributes to impotence—plaguing about seven million men. Some estimates place as many as seventy percent of the cases of damage to penile arteries to "cholesterol-laden macho meals" as *Newsweek* called them back in 1991.

The link between meat eating and impotence catalyzed this ad from People for the Ethical Treatment of Animals:

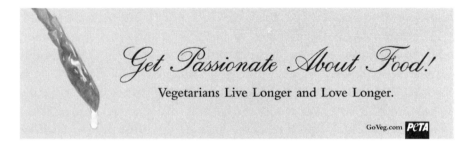

Whether it is this PETA ad or the kitchen debates, male identification is the driving force. As historian Elaine May points out, Krushchev and Nixon weren't arguing about "missiles, bombs, or even modes of government. . . . For Nixon, American superiority rested on the ideal of the suburban home, complete with modern appliances and distinct gender roles for family members."

For women, the public sphere is contaminated by reminders that their distinct gender roles are still in place. From advertisements to ostensibly objective newspaper stories, women's role is as sexual beings, whose availability to men should be their main concern.

A script reasserted in ads, in conversations, in sexual practice:

Privilege. Power. Freedom. The image of the male meat eater embodies all of these.

Subordination. Inequality. Thingification. The image of the consumable woman/animal embodies all of these.

The elevation of the one requires the degradation of the other.

As the kitchen debate suggested, as Abigail Cathcart learned, as Hooters reiterates, as the men's clubs remind women: your role in public life is contingent, not absolute. Why? Because we need you to be some*thing* so we can know we are some*one*.

4

Yoked Oppressions

IN *CULTURE AND THE AD*, William O'Barr notes that hierarchy, dominance, and subordination are the most frequently depicted qualities of social relationships in advertisements. Rarely are ads egalitarian. Ads *advance* someone over something.

The hierarchy that advertisements re-present to us is one in which individuals are associated with groups that are dominant or subordinate.

A = Dominant	Not A = Subordinate
MAN/male	woman/female
CULTURE	nature
HUMAN	animal
"WHITE"	people of color
MIND	body

The Not-A side is defined as being *Not A*, that is

not man: woman
not culture: nature
not human: animal
not white: "colored"
not mind: body

Our luggage is so advanced, you don't have to be.

Making travel less primitive.™

Even though humans are animals, culture arises from nature, nature is known and structured through culture, men and women are overwhelmingly similar, and there is no historical or biological reason to believe that there is a true "white" or true "black"; these dualisms impose an order on our world that we experience as "true," as "real."

The luggage advertisement depicts "Not-A" status: not man, not white, not human, not civilized, not culture.

Dualisms in our culture are not only oppositional—either *this* or *that*, either *A* or *Not-A*. Dualisms are hierarchical, *this* over *that*, *A* over *Not-A*. When the Constitution of the United States bestowed rights only upon those who were completely defined by the "A" side of the dualism (white, human, males, property-owners) it was an acknowledgment of a hierarchy of status, class, and power.

Rationality became associated with being male and human and white. Linked with women, people of color, animals and nature, feelings became suspect. One reason "sympathy" has faced a difficult time being recognized as an ethical position is its association with the body and with women.

As the advertisement for luggage proclaims, disowning our animal connections is part of dominance. The human transcends animality. But Western philosophy defined humanness not only as *not animal*, but also as *not woman*.

From Aristotle forward, the conception of "manhood," the public, civic man, depended heavily on seeing women not merely as lesser humans than men but as less-than-human. This clarifies the exasperation and confusion of many men when women agitated to be included in the Constitution through the woman suffrage amendment: "why, you might as well propose that a cow could vote."

Manhood excludes nonhumans and women.

When Andrea Dworkin comments that "pornography uses those who in the United States were left out of the Constitution," she is reminding us that manhood continues to construct itself through dominance and exclusion.

In *Being and Nothingness,* Sartre shows something more: not just exclusion, but transcendence. For Sartre, transcendence is a project of the masculine and a sign of masculinity. And what is being transcended? Everything the female body is seen as representing—the filth of nature, "holes" and "slime," the inauthentic. Historian Bonnie Smith points out that "Sartre could explain the main point of phenomenology only as the work of a male subject needing to annihilate female subjectivity."

And how does Sartre describe this annihilation?

It is a soft, yielding action, a moist and feminine sucking. . . . In one sense it is like the supreme docility of the possessed, the fidelity of a dog that gives itself.

Two behinds wagging in greeting, two beings tethered to their "masters," two beings about to be taught "obedience," two beings content

with their status. All these doublings of woman and a dog confirm the idea that women are to be mastered, as does the relaxed, "ho-hum" expression on her master.

With the "Obedience School" cartoon, we see *the supreme docility of the possessed, the fidelity of a dog that gives herself.*

A most prosaic example of A/Not-A, shows the hierarchy that is gender:

A	Not A
Mr. John Smith.	*Mrs.* John Smith.

Mrs. John Smith is definitely Not-A, not *Mr.* John Smith; her identity is subsumed under his.

In 1884, Henry James wrote to William Dean Howells, "We talk of you and Mrs you." More recently, the message of the total absorption of the wife's identity into the life of her husband was brought home to one couple. Though they informed social acquaintances that she had kept her own name, still she would be called, "*Mrs.* Smith." Meanwhile her husband would be asked, "Is that *Dr.* John Smith or *Mr.* John Smith?"

People were more concerned about getting *his title* right than about getting *her name* right: You and Mrs. You. They experienced his *someoneness*, but only her *somethingness*.

The other side of the construction of woman as desiring to be controlled is the construction of human male identity as the one who has control.

Chick-fil-A Chargrilled Sandwich

Not only do advertisements appeal to the appetite and say, "We can meet it!" they create anxieties and then say, "We can address them!"

Our culture's anxiety about clear delineations around gender and species is quite apparent through the screen of advertisements. Advertisements maintain a dominance that they depict as difference. Pink and blue blankets at birth are truly only the beginning.

The Chick-fil-A "It's a Grill" campaign featured white words against a pink background, announcing a new "grilled" chicken. The day the campaign was launched, the franchises were decorated with pink balloons and some handed out cigars to surprised customers.

The color pink suggests not only a baby girl—delicate, soft, tender—but a white women (called "pink toes" in *Black Talk*). White women straddle the categories of A/Not-A. In cases of such straddling, generally the "Not-A" associations will be manifest in one way or another, and through those associations womanness ("Not-A" identity) will trump whiteness ("A" identity).

As with the obedience-school cartoon, the presence of a nonhuman summons the reminder that women are animal-like. Make it a snake or other reptile and we know that the advertisement is drawing upon some pretty intense mythic ideas.

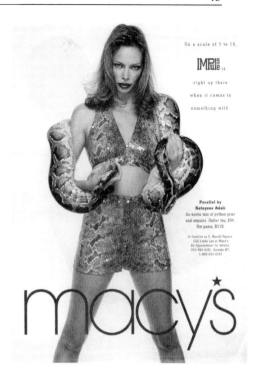

Eve's trespass in eating the fruit off of the tree of good and evil is perhaps the most famous act of consumption in the Western world, one instigated by a snake. And since it is only out of Eden that humans become eaters of animal food, and women become "subject to men," the presence of a snake with a woman provides a potent symbolic reminder of the biblical justification for social dominance.

Women's bodies in the Christian tradition have been deeply connected to images of sin, sex, and death. According to the Bible, the fall of *mankind* and the introduction of death is blamed on a woman and a nonhuman, a snake. As nineteenth century feminist philosopher Elizabeth Cady Stanton declares about the myth of the fall of "Man": "Take the snake, the fruit-tree and the woman from the tableau and we have no fall, nor frowning Judge, no Inferno, no everlasting punishment—hence no need of a Savior. Thus the bottom falls out of the whole Christian theology."

It was *man*, not woman, who was given the power to name women and the other animals.

For many centuries negative attitudes toward sexuality have been expressed by viewing sex as something that resulted from one's base instincts, that is, as something that reduced a human being to an animal. During the Middle Ages—when capital punishment was prescribed for both the non-human and the human involved in bestiality—many people believed that it was the serpent in the Garden of Eden who had introduced Eve to sex. This belief led to a debate about whether Eve and the serpent had actually had intercourse, and left the strong impression that sexual intercourse itself was bestial. Acting sexually was thus considered acting like an animal.

This attitude is evident today when aggressive sexual behavior is referred to as "bringing out the beast" or "wolfish behavior" or "animal passions." One reason the missionary position was trumpeted as *the* position for intercourse was because it was accomplished face-to-face rather than face-to-back, as most nonhumans performed it. It also literally enacted male dominance over the female by the physical positioning of the male body over the female body.

Pornography positions snakes over women's bodies in many poses:

A snake's mouth touching a woman's lips.

A snake touching a woman's labia.

A huge, thick, sinuous snake curling around LaToya Jackson when she appeared in *Playboy*.

The pornographic scenario of Eve and the snake manifests itself not only in advertising. It is a fundamental tenet of a neo-Nazi, anti-Semitic group of white supremacists whose leader, Mark Thomas, teaches a doctrine called "Christian Identity." This hate group came under scrutiny when two neo-Nazi skinheads who had spent time with Mr. Thomas committed a triple murder.

Thomas's "ministry for racists" that is preparing them for a "racial holy war" is held at a compound in Pennsylvania. A teenager described the teachings to *New York Times* reporter, Keith Schneider:

"Their whole religion is based mostly on the first chapter in the Bible," the teen-ager said. "Thomas claims that Jewish people are descended from Cain

who was a descendent of the devil snake and Eve. He claims white people are descendants of Abel who was a descendant of Adam and Eve. He claims there are two main races, Jews and white people. Everyone else is classified under beasts of the field."

As well as anti-Semitism, slavery *(beasts of the field)* has been an essential aspect of white identity for several centuries.

Toni Morrison's *Playing in the Dark* observes that whites needed the fact of black slavery to illustrate the meaning of freedom. Enslaved blacks highlighted the freedom of whites; in being "not-free" they were also "not-me." And has "the parasitical nature of white freedom" really disappeared? Pornographic book and magazine titles such as *A Cocksucking Slave, Soul Slave,* or *Slave Stud* suggest not.

A prevalent theme in pornography is portraying African American women in the South during slavery, thus eroticizing the master-slave relationship and recalling a time when the Constitution excluded them. Titles such as *Black Bitch* and *Bound, Gagged, and Loving It* make the racism more, not less, dangerous. They posit that black women have an animalistic sexuality that must be controlled, otherwise they are dangerous.

In *Playboy,* LaToya Jackson was bound with large snakes, white rope, or contained behind bamboo.

Playboy labeled these bondage scenarios FREE AT LAST.

By appropriating Dr. Martin Luther King, Jr.'s, famous speech to refer to Jackson's experience being used in pornography, *Playboy* implied hers was the ultimate freedom: to appear in bondage in *Playboy.* Subtly, too, they suggest, who needs to be included in the Constitution if you are included in pornography?

In showing her as *not-Free,* they also confirmed her as *not-Me,* Not-A.

Race is always an aspect of the dominance pornography is trying to convey. If a black woman is shown it is

because her black skin has a role in the sexual message. If a white woman is shown it is because her white skin (and often long-legged, large-breasted blondness) has a role in the sexual message. If Asian women are shown, it is often to evoke stereotyped notions of their passivity, their ability to display no sign of pain or fear. If Latina women are portrayed, it is to exploit the stereotype of them as hot, wild, insatiable.

Sex tourists who travel to other countries to buy access to women's bodies believe these racialized myths about women. If they are in Southeast Asian countries, they see the women as naturally subservient and quite eager to please them. If they are in the Caribbean or Latin America, those women are seen as animalistic, insatiable. They do not, therefore, see women who are working in prostitution because they need money.

Showing women with nonhumans or showing them *as* animals is one way to convey that women are animal-like, less than human, unruly, needing to be controlled. Placing them in positions of subservience is another. Implying bestiality, that women are having sex with an animal is another.

Advertisements can only imply, pornography can show.

Today's punks, tomorrow heroes. The basic script of Western culture: the hero and the sex object. A over Not-A.

He is in control. Advertisements designed to show someone in charge may position him upright. In this case, that is not necessary: he is not only above the dominated, but using her, as he, alert, reads. Reading is one of the acts that distinguishes humans from nonhumans.

She is submissive. Irving Goffman notes that advertisements contain rituals of subordination, which involve "lowering oneself physically in some form of prostration"—lying, kneeling, on beds, on floors. This image intensifies the subordination by including the dead bear upon which she, animal-like serves her master.

Catharine MacKinnon says, "Woman through male eyes is sex object, that by which man knows himself at once as man and as subject." Knows himself, actually, as man, as subject, and as human.

A subject is not only male but human.

An object is not only female, but not human.

Yoked together, the Not-A's, the Not-Frees, the Not-Me's, reinforce each other's status as objects.

The dead bear confirms the dominance of the human over the nonhuman. Other "triumphalist" images that proclaim dominance include animal skins, a leather couch, a deer head, or other animals' heads hanging on the wall. Pornography in general naturalizes sexual dominance, making it seem a part of human nature. With nonhumans, or animal skins in the picture, sex, especially *this kind of sex*, looks natural.

When inequality is structured into our lives, it disappears as one of many options for structuring the world and is transformed into a given.

Susanne Kappeler concludes that, "culture, as we know it, is patriarchy's self-image."

And advertising is its self-promotion.

5

Beasts

THIS TOSHIBA AD CAPTURES a prevailing myth of our culture—the natural progression of evolution to its zenith, the white human male. With the white male human body as the prototype, this ad embodies a series of cultural ideas, not only that humans are different from nonhumans, but that men are different from women.

Katherine Frith, in her close examination of this Toshiba ad, wonders whether, if this ad depicted evolution "as beginning with a female and culminating with a fully evolved human woman," would the picture feel right? "Or have we become so used to seeing evolution culminate with a man, that using a woman would seem odd?"

Frith also recognizes the dominance structured into this ad: "the man appears to have dominance over the 'lower' life forms, the apes and the Neanderthal." And what, Frith queries, gives the man his dominance, his superiority? The symbols she sees in the ad are his clothing and his computer. "The assumption in this visual is that man is superior to animals because he has developed socially (clothes) and technologically (tools)."

Despite the fact that technological development has many devastating environmental aspects, the computer in this ad, the symbol of technology, "is depicted as representing the culmination of human evolution and it signifies man's dominance over animals."

Frith finds a further example of dominance in this ad. Clearly, from the clothing the man wears, he is a white-collar worker. The invisible blue-collar worker is not the culmination of evolution; the suit-wearing, upper-class man is.

We might add a few more aspects to the dualistic structure presented to us in the world of advertisements:

A	Not A
MAN/male	woman/female
CULTURE	nature
HUMAN	nonhuman animal
"WHITE"	people of color
MIND	body
CIVILIZED	primitive
PRODUCTION	reproduction
CAPITAL	labor
CLOTHED	naked

Given that these dualisms are structured hierarchically, *the dominated side of the dualism is in service to the dominant*. For instance, in meat production the "Not A" people are the slaughterers. Eighty percent of slaughterhouse jobs are held by immigrants, men of color, and women. Because their employees suffer the highest rate of injury of all jobs, the meat-packing industry has one of the highest worker turnovers.

Most people do not want to be personally responsible for killing. So those with few options in employment do it. As Beverly Smith, an African American feminist health activist told Andrea Lewis, it's not as though the women working in chicken slaughterhouses decided "'I'll go cut up chickens though I could go and be a college professor.'"

When Toshiba changed its advertisement to enclose its message of the myth of evolution within a computer screen, it echoed a change in viewpoint that occurred in early modern Europe: mechanism—the belief that the world was a machine—became a worldview. Mechanism reordered reality around order and power and sanctioned the management of both nature and society.

FARM

Like chickens dispatched by a machine, nature was in Carolyn Merchant's words, "rendered effectively dead, inert and manipulable from without."

Then, in the late nineteenth century, the assembly line became that which manipulates nature and the worker.

Henry Ford credited the idea of the assembly line to the overhead trolley that Chicago meatpackers used in dressing beef: slaughtered animals, suspended head downward, passed from one workman to another and another.

Ford reversed the outcome of the process of slaughtering so that, on the assembly line, a product is created rather than fragmented. Yet in doing so he dismembered the meaning of work, introducing productivity without the sense of being productive.

Carolyn Merchant identifies another consequence of a mechanistic worldview that resulted

FARM

in *The Death of Nature:* "As the unifying model for science and society, the machine has permeated and reconstructed human consciousness so totally that today we scarcely question its validity."

A *New York Times* reporter worked in a slaughterhouse for a few weeks and described his time there:

LOUIS VUITTON

The conveyor belt always overflows with meat around 1 o'clock. So the workers double their pace, hacking pork from shoulder bones with a driven single-mindedness. They stare blankly, like mules in wooden blinders, as the butchered slabs pass by.

It is called the picnic line: 18 workers lined up on both sides of a belt, carving meat from the bone. Up to 16 million shoulders a year come down that line here at the Smithfield Packing Co., the largest production plant in the world. That works out to about 32,000 a shift, 63 a minute, one every 17 seconds for each worker for eight and a half hours a day. The first time you stare down at that belt you know your body is going to give in way before the machine ever will. . . .

The first thing you learn in the hog plant is the value of a sharp knife. The second thing you learn is that you don't want to work with a knife. Finally you learn that not everyone has to work with a knife. Whites, blacks, American Indians and Mexicans, they all have their separate stations.

The few whites on the payroll tend to be mechanics or supervisors. As for the Indians, a handful are supervisors; others tend to get clean menial jobs like warehouse work. With few exceptions, that leaves the blacks and Mexicans with the dirty jobs at the factory, one of the only places with a 50-mile radius in this muddy corner of North Carolina where a person might make more than $8 an hour. . . .

Slaughtering swine is repetitive, brutish work, so grueling that three weeks on the factory floor leave no doubt in your mind about why the turnover is 100 percent. Five thousand quit and five thousand are hired every year. You hear people say, "They don't kill pigs in the plant, they kill people."

Or perhaps they kill both.

Is it imaginable to replace the white, suit-wearing man, carrying a Toshiba computer with a black man or black woman? Katherine Frith poses the question, "Could the culmination of the evolutionary process really be a black man?"

FRED R. CONRAD, *NEW YORK TIMES*

Certainly the racists who accosted Dick Gregory could not imagine such a thing. He describes what happens in his autobiography *Nigger*:

Last time I was down South I walked into this restaurant, and this white waitress came up to me and said: "We don't serve colored people here." I said, "That's all right, I don't eat colored people. Bring me a whole fried chicken." About that time these three cousins come in, you know the ones I mean, Ku, Kluck, and Klan, and they say: "Boy, we're givin' you fair warnin'. Anything you do to that chicken, we're gonna do to you." About then the waitress brought me my chicken. . . . So I put down my knife and fork, and I picked up that chicken, and I kissed it.

Put Rocky in a meat locker and you have the icon of the determined male fighter, of man over nature. But put an African American man in that same meat locker, and the icon is not so undilutedly celebratory. It reinforces the idea of the black man as animal-like and violent.

Advertisements that feature African American men depict them not only as athletes (a very popular theme), but as successful athletes in sports associated with force, like boxing or football, rather than with non-contact sports associated with intellectual skills.

In 1917, H. R. Hopps created an enlistment poster for the US Army that depicted the German enemy as a "brute" (from the Middle English for *nonhuman*, from the Latin for *stupid)*. The German brute is a canine-toothed gorilla, attacking the helpless white, breast-exposed woman.

There he is: the beastly carnivore and his white female meat.

There she lies: vulnerable, innocent, delicate, fragile, white Beauty, in the hands of the primitive Black Beast.

Ostensibly about patriotism, this image contained a thoroughly American story within it as well.

After slavery, the image of blacks changed from that of children needing to be guided and controlled by a benevolent white to dangerous animals, beasts needing to be hunted down and destroyed. Once freed from slavery (postulated as a "civilizing" force), blacks, especially black men were said to be degenerating, becoming uncivilized. This "degeneration" was proof that black men had failed to adapt to freedom.

At the turn of the twentieth century, the Negro was described in the words of one white racist as "a fiend, a wild beast, seeking whom he may devour." Another luridly described the black man's supposed rapist tendencies: ". . . when a knock is heard at the door [the Southern woman] shudders with nameless horror. The black brute is lurking in the dark, a monstrous beast, crazed with lust. His ferocity is almost demoniacal. A mad bull or a tiger could scarcely be more brutal."

For novelist Thomas Dixon, when a black man raped a white woman it was "A single tiger spring, and the black claws of the beast sank into the soft white throat."

In 1915, D. W. Griffith based *The Birth of a Nation* on Dixon's books. Griffith's technological achievement—the first full-length movie—was also an achievement for white racism.

Griffith created the film stereotype of the "pure Black buck." As film his-

LOUIS VUITTON

torian Donald Bogle describes them, "Bucks are always big baadddd niggers, over-sexed and savage, violent and frenzied as they lust for white flesh."

Bucks originally were adult male deers, antelopes, or rabbits.

By 1917, and the appearance of the recruitment poster, nearly 3,000 blacks had been lynched. Less than twenty percent of the time, black men were accused of rape. But the *idea* of a sex crime against a white woman was a part of the lynching frenzy.

As with much pornography, the white man in the recruiting ad is absent from the "picture" but is actually the motivator.

Lynching was not one act, but a series of acts. Often publicized several days in advance, special excursion trains would provide transportation to the proposed site for the lynching which could involve torture, mutilation, being set afire while alive and being burnt to death (slowly if the whites could control the flames), and the dispersal of body parts as souvenirs afterward.

The public burning of a black was called a "Negro Barbecue."

White women turned out to watch the lynchings, too—hoisting children up to insure they could see it as well.

In the "black man rapes white woman scenario" the violation inherent in the alleged rape was against the white male, who had to assert his right to protect his property—Mrs. You, Daughter You, Sister You. Sometimes white men alleged rape to hide the fact that a white woman had *chosen* to have an African American man as her partner.

Not just the white woman, but the idea of her as pure, virginal, and sexless, had to be protected. Like the threat of lynching in its effect on all blacks, the fear of rape helped to keep white woman subordinate, anxious, dependent. It impugned black women by implying that black men preferred white women over them. And the idea of the black rapist also helped deflect attention from white men who, through rape, were sexually and racially terrorizing black women. The African American woman as victim became invisible.

Rape laws, it is said, were written to protect only white women, not black women, racializing womankind into two hierarchical groups—white property or black whore.

When Susan Estrich was raped in 1974, she was asked by the Boston policemen, "was he a *crow?*" i.e., someone who was black, as in *Jim Crow* laws, as in the crows in the Disney *Dumbo* movie. Not only black, but a stranger. In their books, that was *real rape.*

Kate Clark has analyzed reports about rape in the *Sun*, a tabloid with the largest circulation in the United Kingdom. The *Sun* uses subhuman naming for men who are strangers to their victims, (the "real rapists" in Estrich's terms) and if the victim fits their sense of respectable women (property). These attackers are called *fiend, beast, monster, maniac, "ripper."*

In the United States, too, the "beast" language can be found. The rape and violent beating of a wealthy, white woman jogger in Central Park in 1989 provided the press with a field day for bestializing African American

and Hispanic boys. They were *savage, a roving gang*, a *wolf pack*, she was their *prey*. (Only it turns out she wasn't. In 2002, DNA confirmed that she had been raped by someone other than these young men.)

The idea of "real rape" directs our attention away from the fact that the majority of sexually violent men are not strangers. The most frequent kinds of rapes are intraracial and rapes by someone the woman knows—sexual partners, husbands, ex-husbands, boyfriends, acquaintances, fathers, uncles, grandfathers, coaches, teachers, ministers, priests.

Rapists aren't "beasts" or "animals." Generally, they plan their assaults. They target their victims.

At the point at which humans are being the most deliberate in their actions, we call them "beasts."

The "lower" animals are not "beasts" either, that is, they are not ruthlessly violent. They are not "fiends" lacking in dignity or altruism.

ANIMAL JOURNALS

ANIMAL SEX AMONG BLACK WOMEN
by Spencer Washington

For black men, their male identity—rather than moving along the "A" side to being identified with (white) man, moved downward, crossing the species line. This meant that "man" remained a white identity. To be successful as black men in a dominant white culture required that black men conform themselves to an unthreatening manhood, one which speaks words such as "character" and "initiative." Result? The success of conservative black male elites like Clarence Thomas.

Notice what sort of pornography Thomas discussed that Anita Hill found the most offensive:

I think the one that was the most embarrassing was his discussion of pornography involving these women with large breasts and engaged in a variety of sex with different people or animals. This was the thing that embarrassed me the most and made me feel the most humiliated.

During the lynching terrorism, whites accounted for black men's failure to adapt to freedom by claiming that African American women were sexually insatiable and indiscriminate in sexual partners. Not only were they seen as prostitutes, but also as so lascivious that they desired sex with animals.

Perhaps Thomas used pornography in his relationship with Anita Hill as numerous other men have: as part of what is called "grooming behavior." The purpose of grooming behavior is to lower the defenses of the targeted woman: "Look, here, look at what this woman enjoys doing."

LOUIS VUITTON

Grooming behavior is a reminder of the deliberate nature of sexual exploitation and violation. It isn't "bestial" or "animalistic"; it is human and planned.

Ironically, Justice Clarence Thomas could claim "high tech lynching," when in fact the people who were supporting him, conservative whites, were the ones who would have most likely been part of a lynch mob one hundred years ago. His intellectual position was not antagonistic to theirs, or disrespectful of whites. He invoked the term when his political troubles were largely from blacks uninspired by his pedestrian legal career and distrustful of his ideological conservatism, not from whites. Moreover, he implied that the word of a black woman could get him lynched, when no black man was ever lynched on the word of a black woman. (He failed to remind us that black women, too, were lynched.)

A final question the Toshiba ad poses is *Does a capitalist society require a culture based on images?* Mass production enables and requires mass consumption. Henry Ford's most far-reaching contribution to modern life was not just the creation of a new type of worker, but a new type of human—the modern consumer.

A man within a computer carrying a computer home. With this Toshiba image resides one last connection. John Tierney explained it for the readers of the *New York Times*: "Men are the chief consumers of porn, and men are also the main enthusiasts for new communication gadgets. This means, for instance, that the markets for the first home movie projectors or CD-ROM drives have conveniently overlapped with the market for pornography." The term "killer ap" refers to that function of a new technology that makes it appealing. For CD-ROMS, pornography has been the killer ap.

What else besides a vast amount of entertainment will stimulate and anesthetize the injuries of class and race? Clarence Thomas provides an answer: *pornography involving these women with large breasts and engaged in a variety of sex with different people or animals.*

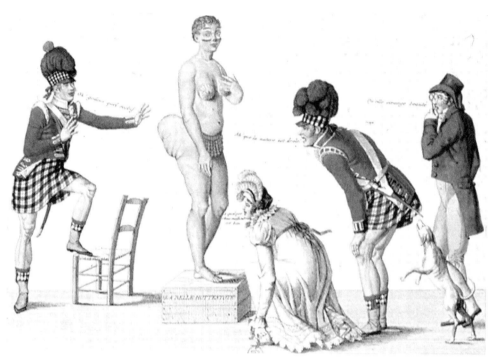

Les Curiex en extase ou les cordons de souliers *(1814)*
Courtesy of the Bibliotheque nationale de France, Paris

6

Hamtastic

PATRICIA HILL COLLINS, an African American feminist, proposes that pornography as we know it now developed based on black women's association with nonhuman animals' bodies.

Collins discusses the case of Saartjie Bartmann, a young Khoisan woman. (Khoisans were the first inhabitants of South Africa pejoratively labeled "Hottentots.") Only 4′6″ tall, Bartmann was exhibited in England and France while alive, and once dead, she was dissected. Known as the "the Hottentot Venus" by the dominant (white) culture, Europeans were fascinated with her "protruding buttocks" and her genitalia. They glimpsed the first, but until her death, could only fantasize about the second.

In this sketch—*The Curious in Ecstasy or the Laces of Shoes*—a French artist is mocking how the British responded to Bartmann (whose name underwent a change). "Ah, how amusing nature is!" one soldier exclaims. Peering through lorgnettes, the civilian male asserts, "What strange beauty!" The woman bending down to tie her shoes rejoices that "From some points of view misfortune can be good." Her gaze is taking in the kilted man on the left. And he is reaching to touch Bartmann's buttocks exclaiming, "Oh, goddam what roast beef!"

She wasn't just "meat," she was, *roast* beef, i.e., "the beef that built an empire" of the British Beefeaters.

Scotland is the home both of beef production and kilted men. Its relationship to beef production is still felt today. According to vegetarian historian Rynn Berry, "Commerical cattle ranching in the US was organized and financed by Scottish banks, and the largest cattle ranches in the United States are still owned by families of Scottish descent."

The dog's presence functions to represent animality, bestiality, "unbridled" sexuality. But is the dog, with his face to the rear of another kilt-clad soldier, imitating the humans, or are they imitating the dog?

From the seventeenth century forward, to "beat the dog" was to masturbate.

And though this French image attempts to make fun of the British way of looking at her, she was exhibited in France as well. This time by an *animal trainer;* for three francs one could view her and a male rhinoceros. And though she most probably was never exhibited nude (the color of her clothing matched her skin color), it is the French artist who undresses her—to expose her buttocks—a reminder that all images of her represent the point of view of the dominant culture.

In the hierarchical Great Chain of Being, whites were at the top, and "Hottentots" were thought to be the lowest of all human species, nearer to apes. Were they the missing link that straddled the boundaries between human and apes? At least one group of Europeans on a hunting expedition in Africa must have thought not, as they shot and ate a "Hottentot."

Bartmann's racial identity allowed her to be displayed. Her near nakedness sexualized her, and speculation about her genitalia provided a focus and excuse for drawing racist and sexist conclusions—about an inherently deviant black female sexuality and unredeemable primitive racial type.

The specific interest was with her protruding buttocks and the labia minora. Also known as the *nymphae,* they are, as Pulitzer Prize–winning reporter Natalie Angier describes them in *Woman: An Intimate Geography,* "the exquisite inner origami of flesh that enfolds the vagina and nearby urethral opening." It was thought that Bartmann, like other Khoisan women, had a hypertrophied or overdeveloped *nymphae,* and so the flap of skin that covered her genitalia was known as the "Hottentot apron." (In fact, it was a medical myth.)

She was seen as both savage and bestial.

The late Stephen Jay Gould points out that this is curious. Her sexual organs, rather than being seen as proof of her "animality," should instead

PENNY SIOPIS, *DORA AND THE OTHER WOMAN*

have been seen as the exact opposite: "Humans are the most sexually active primates, and humans have the largest sexual organs of our order. In this dubious line of argument a person with a larger than average endowment is, if anything, more human."

But that is not how Europeans saw it in 1815.

Scientific racism appeared just when slavery was being debated. For many whites, the idea of black freedom threatened social stability. (Recall Toni Morrison's insight that white ideas of freedom required someone else who was both *not free* and *not me.*) If Bartmann's genitalia were sufficiently different, this would confirm that blacks were a lower race in the Great Chain of Being. So blacks, even if they were no longer *not free* would still remain *not me.*

White "freaks" were *oddities* of their race; blacks on display were seen as *typical* of their race.

When Bartmann died, she was dissected by Baron Cuvier and Henride Blainville. They wanted to get their hands on her sexual organs to see if they could determine from that if she were human or nonhuman. When he had observed her alive, Cuvier had believed her movements were like those of a monkey, thinking she pushed out her lips like an orangutan. And though he and his men had hoped to see her genitals, she kept a handkerchief covering them.

To see her as "ape-like" he discounted the evidence that she knew three languages.

When dead she could not talk back, nor keep her genitalia covered.

And when he was done dissecting her, Cuvier conserved her brain and genitalia—in full labia display—in bottles of formaldehyde. They remained there until 2002, when they were finally returned, along with her skeleton, to South Africa.

According to Londa Schiebinger in *Nature's Body,* eighteenth century illustrators depicted the "Hottentot" woman from the front to show her "apron." Nineteenth century illustrators showed her from the back, to highlight her "buttocks."

Later, such buttocks became associated with prostitutes. Sexist science became attracted to the "abnormal" labia of prostitutes which supposedly represented a more primitive structure, too.

After the dissection, especially with her genitals in formalin, and a cast of her body on display, viewers could encounter both Bartmann's buttocks and her nymphae.

Sarah Bartmann had truly been reduced to her sexual parts.

In 1869, the "bustle" was invented allowing middle and upper class white women to accentuate *their* backsides.

With Sarah Bartmann, the public display of a woman's sexualized, racialized, animalized nude fragmented body became legitimate. Here pornography as we know it could be said to originate. All of the Not-A associations prevailed.

Her humanness, like that of all women of color, firmly grounds her on the "A" side, and so intensifies the assaultive nature of the bestializing constructions.

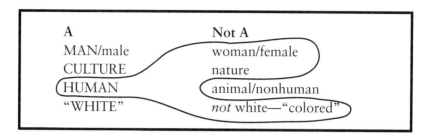

White men knew that African American women were not *really* nonhuman animals—they were the ones who were raping them, and they did not see themselves as bestialists.

Collins, the theorist, continues in her analysis of pornography drawing on the work of Scott McNall. By using "rear-entry position photographs. . . . All of these kinds of photographs reduce the woman to her reproductive system, and furthermore, make her open, willing, and available—not in control. . . ."

Black women's bodies had been reduced to sexual parts: a womb, for reproduction; a vagina, for rape; genitals, for speculation about deviant sexuality. Black women were exploited as "breeders" like female nonhumans; raped and yet the word "rape" was not invoked for their experience of sexual violation; displayed on the auction block of slavers, as white men made money off of their bodies. All of these reasons lead Collins to conclude that pornography became the pornography as we know it now because of the

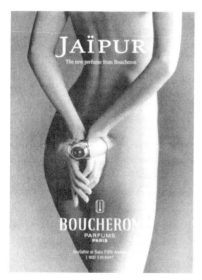

historic treatment of black women: black women were not added into a preexisting pornography. Instead, pornography "must be reconceptualized as a shift from the objectification of Black women's bodies in order to dominate them, to one of media representations of all women that perform the same purpose."

Chains, whips, wrist clasps (bracelets?), ropes—all forms of capture, bondage, and control (of both human slaves and all nonhumans) are reminders that black women were seen as animal-like. The racial dynamics may fade from view, (just as the skin color did in those quadroon and octoroon enslaved women who had been bred to be light—white—yet sexually available like whores, "slave mistresses" for the white master).

In chapter 4, "Yoked Oppressions," it was noted how the dualistic differences of the A side and the Not-A side are hierarchical. As with the Great Chain of Being, someone is up and someone else is down.

In the preceding chapter, "Beasts," we learned of another quality of these dualisms—Not-A's *serve* A's.

The inequality of the Not-A side has one further dimension to it: this "colored"/animal/female side is in sexualized service to the white male side. Inequality is made sexy.

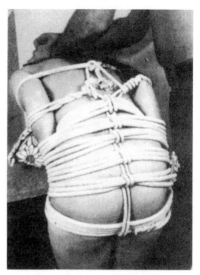

From Diana E. H. Russell,
Against Pornography

Slavery was never an "idea" separate from actions. Sarah Bartmann's body was never an "idea." And neither is pornography as we know it.

The terms for discussing pornography as though it is speech were in place before pornography as we know it came into existence. Pornography became a record of *acts* done to women's bodies first in slavery, and then through photography, film, video, and digital media. But pornography as we debate it (as speech) is not pornography as we know it (acts based on inequality).

The pornographer's freedom, like the pornography users', requires women's lack of freedom.

Women's harm becomes men's pleasure. Domination over women becomes experienced and expressed sexually.

Museum officials in France who exhibited Sarah Bartmann's labial display, and the plaster body molding that had been made of her, learned exactly how women's harm becomes men's pleasure. Museum visitors became aroused seeing the remnants of her body. T. Denean Sharpley-Whiting explains in *Black Venus* that its exhibition was discontinued since "one of the female tour guides was allegedly accosted, and the molding itself had become the object of touching and many amorous masturbatory liaisons."

When women are shown in positions of bondage, or implied bondage, the message to men is powerfully clear: submission, and subjugation are acceptable; women are powerless and enjoy being powerless; women are

available as the targets of aggression and violence; women are inferior to men; animal-like. The effect of these messages is to confirm that women exist to fulfill the sexual needs of men and deserve to be dominated.

Collins says pornography portrays women as "sexual animals awaiting conquest."

The T-shirt marketed by the "Bovine Club" of Michigan State University's College of Veterinary Medicine depicts rectal palpation, which is done to see if cows are in their estrus cycle and thus ready to be "bred," that is, forcibly impregnated. As every veterinary student would recognize, this act precedes sexually dominating the cow.

What is the message of these rear-entry images? Clearly, the idea of sodomy is invoked. And with sodomy, submissiveness, humiliation, degradation. *Defeat.* For humans, sodomy is a way to subordinate the conquered; it has been used by the victors in wars against both males and females.

Sodomy is also linked to the presumption about how other animals "do" it. By its association with nonhumans, it becomes taboo-ed. (Taboo-ed, too, because homosexual men are assumed to have sex in this way.)

Taboo-breaking and domination become linked in this basic rear-entry positioning of women.

Commenting on the surprising number of women they interviewed who had been anally raped by their husbands, two experts observe:

Raping a woman anally was an act by which the men expressed their anger, their control, and their desire to punish. . . . The act in itself, when imposed by force, emphasizes the passivity, subservience, and impersonality of the victim. . . . Because the man is facing the woman's back, he can avoid confronting her feelings and reactions. . . . He can treat her as an impersonal object. In many ways, anal rape appears to be the quintessential way for a man to humiliate his wife.

It was claimed that Bartmann had consented to being on display. A signed contract was offered as proof—a contract, it is speculated, which came into existence only when proof of her consent was demanded.

The idea of consent presumes that the equality that we are working for has already been achieved.

Or as Andrea Dworkin more pointedly reminds us, "If you can force a woman to fuck a dog, you can force a woman to sign a contract."

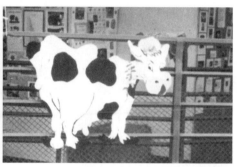

"The girls at the club have become my friends. I love to party with them after dancing, and shopping on the upper West Side or the Village."

"I've met some pretty hot guys at the club. I received two marriage proposals and one guy went as far as buying me a puppy."

CATHY GOEGGEL

BIG   ASS
PRIME RIB FRI

GROUPER WED
ALL U CAN EAT
1.00 DRAFTS

DAVID DEL PRINCIPE

Any construction that wants to show a woman as sexually available may opt to put her on all fours. Collins continues in her analysis, quoting Scott McNall: rear-entry photographs tell us women "are animals because they are the same as dogs—bitches in heat who can't control themselves."

Just how did Cuvier describe Bartmann's genitalia, the "Hottentot apron," which he dissected?

The apron . . . is a development of the nymphae. . . . The outer lips, scarcely pronounced, were intercepted by an oval of four inches; from the upper angle descended between them a quasi-cylindrical protuberance of around eighteen lines long and over six lines thick, whose lower extremity enlarges, splits, and protrudes like two fleshly, rippled petals of two and a half inches in length and roughly one inch in width. Each one is rounded at the tip; their base enlarges and descends along the internal border of the outer lip of its side and changes into a fleshy crest. . . . If one assembles these two appendages, together they form a heart-shaped figure . . . in which the middle would be occupied by the vulva.

Ruth's Chris Steak House later changed the words that accompany their labial display to COME HUNGRY.

By sexualizing dominance, pornography and advertising take it to another level. They make it fun.

A woman heard a man proclaim loudly to his companion, "I want me a piece of that." When she looked up expecting to see someone carrying a cake, she realized that they were pointing at and talking about her.

CAROL J. ADAMS

Another woman tells this story:

So I tell them, "Look. You look like nice guys. But it's not nice to comment on me like I'm just part of the scenery. I'm here for my own purposes. OK?"

One answered, "You know you're just a piece of meat to me, bitch."

7

Body Chopping

JO SPENCE/TERRY DENNETT, *STILL LIFE*

When asked about their sexual fantasies, many men describe scenes of disembodied, faceless body parts: breasts, legs, vaginas, buttocks.

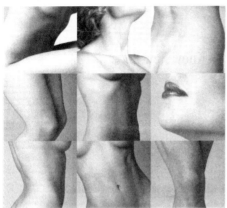

If you think she's got it all,
you should see what she's missing.

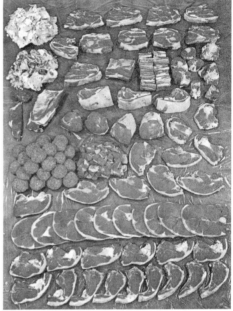

SINCLAIRVILLE CUSTOM MEAT CUTTING
"Our Guarantee — You Get All Your Own Meat Back"
22 Park St.
Sinclairville, N.Y. 14782
Phone — Tom Peck — 962-4242

IN ADVERTISING, *body chopping* is a formal term for images that display only a part of an individual. Advertisers dismember body parts to enhance the effectiveness of an ad—at least that is the ostensible reason for depicting a shoulder or a leg rather than an entire body.

Ads often depict women's bodies without heads, faces or feet. Less frequently, men are depicted in this manner. These advertisements declare that all that truly matters about a woman is between her neck and her knees.

An average meat eater will consume in his or her lifetime: 984 chickens, 37 turkeys, 29 pigs, 12 cattle, two lambs, one calf and more than 1,000 fishes.

T-shirts for sale
Washington, D.C., 2001

MOLLY HATCHER

Joby Warrick of the *Washington Post* described the work of body chopping:

It takes 25 minutes to turn a live steer into steak at the modern slaughterhouse where Roman Moreno works. For 20 years, his post was "second-legger," a job that entails cutting hocks off carcasses as they whirl past at rate of 309 an hour.

The cattle were supposed to be dead before they got to Moreno. But too often they weren't.

"They blink. They make noises," he said softly. "The head moves, the eyes are wide and looking around."

Still Moreno would cut. On bad days, he says, dozens of animals reached his station clearly alive and conscious. Some would survive as far as the tail cutter, the belly ripper, the hide puller. "They die," said Moreno, "piece by piece."

In the view of the young writer who penned the following words, the animals are mass terms of meat before they are even dead.

The enemy is upon us. We respond with speed and fury, with all the might of technology and greed on our side, but no matter what we do, they won't stop coming. We cut off their feet, their ears, and their heads we split their carcasses in 2 and grind up their insides for our children to eat at baseball games. Pieces of the enemy are everywhere—on chains, on belts, hanging from the ceiling on hooks, but the message is apparently not getting out in this nightmare, for every one we kill, there is one more to take its place.

His specific job was as a "rounds puller"—a body-chopper who separates the stomach from the intestines, empties the intestines, and amputates the colon. Verbs are all that are necessary to describe his work: "Lift. Slash. Grab. Sever. Heave. Squeeze. Slice. Rinse, Repeat."

Parts are less than the whole. A whole person has autonomy and individuality. A woman severed into sexualized body parts cannot be whole or au-

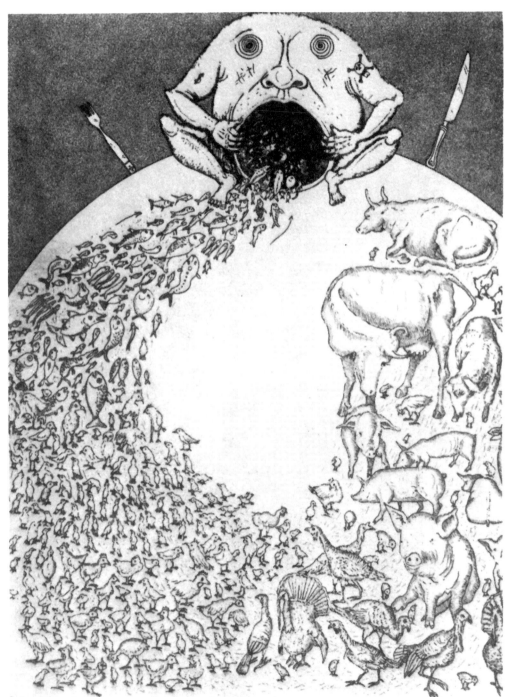

In ten years the average American consumes— 144 fishes, 185 chickens, 8 turkeys, 7 pigs, 1 lamb, 2 cows

SUE COE

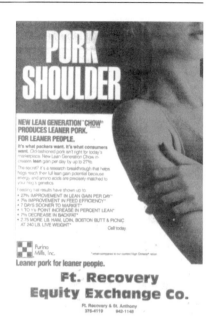

tonomous or an individual. Humiliation and degradation don't matter as much if there is no "individual" being injured, no one to object or to scream.

In the face of faceless body parts, no one exists to be asked, "what are you going through?" "What are you feeling?"

Meat companies, newspaper illustrators, advertisers, and restaurant owners show us how pornography works to construct "consumable" women by using those constructs to promote their product—a sliced, slashed, dead body part.

Again advertisements suggest, pornography portrays: women not only *have* "cunts" they *are* cunts that exist for male masturbation. In the book *Backstreets*, a prostitute's vagina is described "as a garbage can for hordes of anonymous men's ejaculations." Prostitutes evolve a survival strategy for differentiating parts of the self that are available for sexual consumption. "The vagina is rented out. But

Just what Miami needs.
more breasts and thighs.

World Cuisine at China Grill.
Open now for previews
in Miami Beach.

CHINA GRILL

60 W. 53rd St., New York City
Lunch•Dinner•Late Supper
212-333-7788
404 Washington Ave., Miami Beach
Dinner•Late Supper
305-534-2211

nothing more. You never get my thoughts. Not my mind, not my soul, not my mouth. There's something that is mine alone and that you'll never get hold of. I'm not really there."

With this division, they can protect parts of themselves from destruction. Their day-to-day survival requires the long-term rendering of their humanity; a fragmented being can face the day's work.

According to my *Dictionary of Euphemisms*, "piece" means "a female viewed sexually by a male." *Piece* is how women are treated by sexual harassers who call out to them, "Look at them legs" or "Hey whore" or "wanna fuck?" or "fucking cunt."

When Hillary Clinton was First Lady, a Fort Worth restaurant offered a "Hillary Dinner": "two fat thighs, two small breasts, and a left wing." Recently this image started circulating on the Internet, though probably not an actual photograph of a KFC franchise, still a reminder that regardless of achievement (Senator or the First Lady of the United States), any woman can be reduced to her sexual parts.

Talking about women's body parts is a way to assert male heterosexuality. By body chopping a woman, a man can position himself as a successful sexual predator in the eyes of his peers.

Rudolph's Barbeque is one of the few ads that also appeared in a gay newspaper, with two men depicted. That the dominant perspective can move with some adjustment into a homosexual context has been problematic for the gay community, where meat can also be used as a vehicle for power. The language of gay culture is notable for referring to older, traditionally masculine men as "bears" or "wolves," and younger men/boys as "chicken" and "lambs." During the early part of the twen-

tieth century, sailors—a fetishized group for gay men—were referred to as "seafood." Young Marines and Navy men are referred to as "tuna" (the chicken of the sea).

Wolves, in fact, are faithful; they mate for life; they are affectionate parents and loyal to their pack.

Machismo eating is a term applied by *New Yorker* writer Joan Acocella, who describes her ex-husband's willingness to eat the *obvious* parts of a body: the neck, the tail, the toes, the head. She writes that,

he had a weakness for food machismo—that is, he prided himself on eating what you wouldn't. Tripe was nothing to him; he ate necks, tails, toes. One of the things he loved best was when we were out to dinner with friends and someone confessed an unwillingness to eat certain animal parts. Then he would tell the story of how the biggest treat in his grandfather's house was capuzzell, *or sheep's head. They would take this head, roast it, and hoist it out onto a platter. Then Grandpa would crack it open. ("Stop! Stop!" we're all yelling at my husband by now. But there was no stopping him.) Grandpa would crack it open and then stick in the spoon and scoop out ("No! Please!")—Grandpa would scoop out the brains onto everyone's plate. The people who were really lucky got the ("No, Nick! Don't tell us!")—the people who were lucky got the eyeballs. The story thus triumphantly finished, our dinner companions would look down glassy-eyed at their plates, push them away, and order a drink.*

SUBSTANTIAL SANDWICHES

HELEN'S GRILLED CHICKEN SANDWICH
Marinated & grilled breast of chicken topped with Swiss cheese,
avocado, red onion, tomato, sprouts, & our own honey-mustard sauce,
between 2 slices of rosemary-parmesan bread. $6.50

UNCOMMON VEGGIE SANDWICH
So much stuff you won't miss the meat!
Cukes, zukes, avocado, tomato, onion, peppers, mushrooms &
sprouts, with cream cheese on toasted millet bread. · $4.95

"DOUBLE D CUP" BREAST OF TURKEY
This sandwich is so BIG... Just checking to see if you really read the menu!
Freshly cut whole breast of turkey on toasted millet bread with
walnut cream cheese, cranberries, lettuce & sprouts... Gobble, Gobble! $6.25

DOLPHIN-SAFE TUNA SANDWICH
We could NEVER condone hurting dolphins, so we use all white meat
Chicken of the Sea in our tasty tuna salad. It's served on millet toast with
lettuce, tomato & sprouts. $4.95
Try it with "Homemade Pesto" for .75 extra.
ADD A **CUP OF SOUP** *TO ANY SANDWICH FOR $1.95 PER ORDER*

The menu from Uncommon Grounds in Chicago provides opportunities for sexual harassment over lunch.

First, note that their vegetarian sandwich is "Uncommon." Not just a pun upon their name, they are reminding us that other vegetarian sandwiches, those *common* ones, will make you miss the meat, but not theirs. Placed directly above " 'Double D Cup' Breast of Turkey," draws one's attention quickly away from something uncommon to something common: male humor about women and nonhumans.

In *A History of the Breast,* Marilyn Yalom detects that, "Clothes that come in direct contact with the naked body are often seen as sex objects in their own right, fetishes from the fantasy side of public dress." With this menu item, the bra is a sex object. But there is more.

There is the sexualization of size. The fascination with large breasts and what women have done to achieve them—using push-up bras, silicone implants, surgical augmentation—are all sandwiched by implication into this title. After all, it is a double "D" cup rather than an "A" cup. When a woman's figure before breast-implant surgery has been called "boyish" by the *New York Times*, when the American Society of Plastic and Reconstructive Surgeons during the 1990s called small breasts "deformities," and "a disease which in most patients results in feelings of inadequacy," who would chose to have small breasts or an "A" cup sandwich?

There is also the sexualization of *injuring breasts*, like the *freshly cut* breast in the sandwich. (It is customary in medical schools to cut the breasts off a female cadaver so that the body is more "normal.") In the context of pornographic publications such as *Tit and Body Torture Photos, Big Breast Bondage*, or *Black Tit and Body Torture* this sandwich listing, too, celebrates breast mutilations.

With the "Double D Cup" sandwich, we see the sexualization of eating the injured breast (which is the most profitable cut of "meat" from the turkey). In the pursuit of ever larger "turkey breasts," the size and the shape of turkeys have been altered. Through genetic selection, larger-breasted turkeys have been chosen

Own your own trophy of the world's greatest hunt

Mammalia Americana

New trophy room conversation piece to illustrate the high points of your best adventure story.

Life-like shape. Unbreakable plastic with trophy Bronze finish. Overall size 12 x 10 with nameplate.

ONLY

$5.95
POSTPAID

Satisfaction Guaranteed or Money Back

from an advertisement in *Penthouse*, submitted by Mary Grauerholz, Albany, N. Y.

MS. MAGAZINE

over and over again in breeding, so that turkeys have become top heavy in terms of shape and much larger than normal. They have such huge chests that when they start to approach "slaughter" weight, their legs are unable to hold their bodies up, and their skeletons can't support their body mass. Consequently, they develop leg problems, arthritis, and often fall over. The breasts of both the male and the female are so big that the male cannot mount the female anymore to reproduce.

Even if the turkey being eaten was a male, the human consumer is told they are consuming fragmented female body parts.

Tucked into the menu, just below a sandwich many women might gravitate to (if only because our culture has told them to watch their weight, and this has been equated with vegetarianism), is a reminder to all women that they are in male space, that this man-to-man language about consumption is about them, that they are objects not subjects, that there is no public space uncontaminated by the presumption of accessibility, of human male privilege. Truly, someone's harm has become another's pleasure.

Just *who* has been harmed disappears.

There is no *who*, only a body part, and there is no harm, just a joke and a sandwich.

Gobble. Gobble.

FARM SANCTUARY

Turkeys entering slaughterhouse

8

Armed Hunters

Men who *go grousing,* that is men who are after birds, game hens, game pullets, lone doves, partridges, pheasants, or plovers, are all after the same thing: prostitutes.

> "Call it *Playboy* for deer hunters. Call it serious therapy for the trophy voyeur, the antler impaired. Or call it *Big Rack IV.*"
>
> —review of a book on hunting Texas Whitetail "Bucks"

Many battered women's shelters have refused the offer from hunters of the flesh of nonhuman animals who were hunted down and killed. They have refused not only because some hunters are batterers but because hunting essentially normalizes violence; their residents have been at the receiving end of similar violent behavior.

The gang rape of an unconscious woman is called *beaching;* the woman is like a beached whale.

The cover to a CD by the Harpoons shows a boat full of men, with one standing in the bow throwing a harpoon at a giant inflatable blond white woman lying atop the water. He is aiming it toward her crotch.

"Thar *she* blows."

Why would women's subordinate status be the referent point for a whale? Because, explains André Joly, *she* denotes a *minor power* whereas *he* denotes a *major power*: "Sportsmen, whalers, fishermen are in special relation to the animal. Whatever its size or strength, it is regarded as a potential prey, a power that has to be destroyed—for sport or food—hence a dominated power." Male victims of hunting, like male victims of slaughtering, become symbolically female.

The victim of the hunt is a dominated power within a sexual system that is structured along lines of dominance and subordinance. After Rex Perysian told his hunting pals, "I'll grab it like I grab my women," then, according to the *Philadelphia Inquirer*'s Alfred Lubrano who reported the event, "he

"I'll grab it like I grab my women!" Rex Perysian said of the boar he killed at Renegade Ranch

dropped the animal's head and bellowed into the woods, boasting that the kill had sexually aroused him."

Perysian's success was at a canned hunt. Someone chased the boars along an animal trail toward their breakfast bin, which is why one hunter—who abandoned hunting after experiencing a canned hunt years ago—calls it "like taking a gun to the zoo." (Sometimes the animals have indeed come from the zoos or circuses.)

Despite claims to the contrary, hunting was not central to the emergence of Homo sapiens. The first eaters of non-human-animal protein were not actually hunters bringing the "game" home, but eaters of insect protein and scavengers of animals' bodies left by carnivores. Hunting is even less glamorous now.

Erik Erikson seems to understand how troubling violence against nonhumans is in his remarks in *Gandhi's Truth* that,

> *the eating of animal flesh, an easy matter of course for most people unless made complex by ritual warnings, may yet turn out to be a problem of psycho-social evolution when mankind comes to review and reassess the inner and outer consequences of having assumed the life of an armed hunter, and all the practical and emotional dead ends into which this has led us.*

Canned hunts sometimes involve drugging the nonhumans to make them easier targets or keeping them caged until just before the hunter is reader to shoot. In any case, canned hunts take place on well-fenced land, so that the animals can run but the paths lead only to dead ends. Perysian, despite this setting, required four minutes and three arrows to kill the boar.

Persyian's remarks remind us that the armed hunter is armed most intimately with his own penis. For it is time to address the problem of the "penis." The cock, bone, prick, rod. The penis, as its synonyms suggest, represents the power to penetrate, and this becomes the power at the root of domination. The black man's penis was often attacked and severed by white men during lynching—becoming "the ultimate souvenir."

Castration of male animals is a common action to keep the meat tasty. Historian Philip Dray explains that "The act of castration, a horrifying component of many lynchings, was at least mechanically familiar to most Southern participants, men accustomed to the slaughter of fowl and livestock and such practices as the gelding of horses."

Male testicular anxiety is the term animal shelter workers have for the reluctance of men to neuter their male dogs.

When referring to women, meat refers to all of a woman. She is a piece of meat. For men, meat is his penis. After I showed *The Sexual Politics of Meat Slide Show* on one campus, somebody E-mailed the student organizer of the show a picture of a heavily lipsticked white woman giving a white man fellatio, with the comment, "If you want a piece of meat—I've got a nice, hard piece of meat for you. . . . Love, Max."

One lynch mob forced their victim to eat his own genitals before killing him, an act of self-cannibalism.

Until recently, many insurance programs funded Viagra prescriptions but not birth control.

Fuck, screw, pork—all verbs for the action of the penis in sexual activity. The penis becomes associated with entitlement, power, humanity; the vulva with weakness, powerlessness, with animals.

When a group of animal rights activists protested the organizing of a bullfight in Poland, twelve activists jumped over the fence into the bullring and sat down. Some people in the audience rushed the ring to punch and kick the protestors. One of the toreadors stood in front of a protesting young woman, pulled his pants down, held her head and tried to place it between his legs.

The "cowboy" on the phone, on the following page, was complaining that the bull he had been sent only "covered" five cows.

To produce turkeys, a *Tom milking chair* has been created, a chair used in laboratories to masturbate male turkeys.

CATHY GOEGGEL

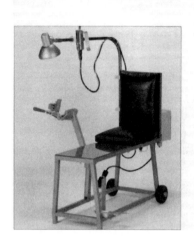

ONE-MAN TOM MILKING BENCH
Patent #3,872,869

With bulls, a plastic vagina is put over the penis so that the bulls can be masturbated into them. Boars, too, are "milked" in this way.

Although it has a potential for much variety, heterosexual sexual activity becomes *something men do to women*. Why has sexual intercourse been reduced to what men do, and thus men's sexual identities become reduced to this organ alone, reduced so utterly that its image must be constantly reiterated through phallic symbols like guns, arrows, knives, scissors, rifles, cattle prods, broom handles, snakes, vacuum cleaners, the pointed phallic hats of the Ku Klux Klan, and the asparagus?

Why does the legal definition of rape—including issues of penetration and "consent"—represent the male perspective?

Though PORK THE ONE YOU LOVE is probably a web-generated image, it follows a trajectory of copulation from a heterosexual-male point of view. Language about sex from this perspective is

SUBJECT   VERB   OBJECT
Man fucks/porks/screws animalized/objectified woman

Language about the hunt is structured in this same way:

SUBJECT   VERB   OBJECT
Man kills/hunts/stalks feminized nonhuman

Pornography is called *stroke books*.

A young woman walking in the woods stumbled upon some hunters. "Here's a live one!" they said, putting aside their pornography, and raped her.

Here's a live one. The issue is not so much the hunting context, though it is telling, but the hunting language, *live one*. Live, not only as opposed to "dead," which could refer to a hunted nonhuman, but also live, as opposed to "inanimate," referring to the objectified woman on the pages before them. Now they had before them a *live objectified woman* and they knew what to do: Subject Verb Object.

Pornography doesn't work if *someone* is there; a woman must not be too real, she must not be equal.

A story from the *Chapel Hill Herald* about a deer who had "evaded a Hillsborough man for years" describes male stalking. BULLWINKLE'S DEATH ENDS BOWHUNTER'S QUEST. We learn in passing that hunting with a bow is quicker, more painless than hunting with a gun ("With a gun, they die from the shock"). But the main story is how this hunter had stalked his prey. Duncan Murrell, the reporter, tells us "for three years the buck eluded him during the hunting season, later revealing himself when the only thing Arnao could shoot him with was a video camera."

This hunter, like many others, now feeds, that is, *baits*, the deer on his land and plants thick patches of clover throughout his property. Murrell, the reporter, admits, "Feeding deer might not sound quite fair to the layman, but it's an increasingly popular practice among hunters who hope to develop land into areas chock-full of trophy bucks."

A review in *The New Yorker* of the restaurant Quilty's described how the chef

is brave, unafraid of game [hunted animals], but she treats it as though it's been seduced rather than shot. Her roasted loin of venison, for instance, is served with a fox-grape poivrade, black-trumpet mushrooms, and a cauliflower gratin—things you might actually feed a deer if you weren't planning on killing it instead.

Or, for that matter, even if you are.

The hunter reports, "I would wake up in a cold sweat thinking about the deer." He continued: "Some people say that I had gotten obsessed, that it's the hardest thing in the world to hunt one animal. . . . I would say I'm not obsessed. I just wanted this animal."

Why, after baiting the deer and naming the deer and recognizing the deer's individuality, did he kill the deer? Answer: *I'm a hunter.*

Hunting's culmination in the killing of an animal reiterates a male orgasm—the tumescence and then the ejaculation, the hunt and then the kill. But other scenarios and attitudes toward the act of heterosexual copulation exist: it could be seen to be *enclosing, surrounding, engulfing.* Meanwhile the existence of multiple orgasms, at least for women, offers a different trajectory than the orgasmic completion through ejaculation or the death of the prey.

Yet we are shackled to a male-biased hydraulic conception of male sexuality: it assumes the explosive nature of male sexuality that needs an outlet, as though sex is an autonomous force, not influenced by culture, not in relationship to all of life.

Martha Vicinus explains the problem with defining sexuality from an "overwhelmingly male and heterosexual" point of view:

In this energy-control (or hydraulic) model, sexuality is seen as an independent force or energy disciplined by personal and social constraints. Sex is always something to be released or controlled; if controlled, it is sublimiated or deflected or distorted. . . . Sexuality in general is defined in terms of the male orgasm; it is like a powerful force that builds up until it is spent in a single ejaculation.

The existence of bestiality—and surely some of the paraphernalia for hunters suggest the nonhuman as a fixated love object—is often justified through this hydraulic model. One form of bestiality is even called *safety-valve sex;* that is, "I need a sexual release. There are no human partners around. A nonhuman animal is available. I'll get it on with that animal."

Safety-valve sex is often cast as a casual act of the curious young, as sexual exploration. The nonhumans they have access to are the animals who will be sexually used: cats, dogs, sheep, cows, hens, rabbits, goats, mules, ducks, rabbits, horses, boars, bull, fishes.

Many forms of sexual contact between humans and nonhuman animals are physically destructive to those animals. Few vaginas, especially those of young animals, are large enough to accommodate the penis of a male Homo sapiens. Small animals may experience torn rectums and internal bleeding after being sexually assaulted, and chickens and rabbits are often killed by the act itself. Sadistic sexual behavior against animals also occurs. Chickens

are frequently decapitated because this intensifies convulsions of the sphincter, thereby increasing the sexual pleasure of the man.

The notion of bestiality as a safety valve that operates until the men are ready for women leads one to ask whether the women to whom these young men graduate are not safety valves, too.

Since it posits a hydraulic system of pent-up energy needing release, hunting reiterates the beliefs about a male sexuality that requires release. The idea of "dominance" disappears as the hunter, in his language, "merges" at the moment of the kill with the hunted.

In *Backstreets*, a "john" describes seeking a prostitute as a hunt:

Men can drive around and maybe feel that they're hunting prey night after night before they shoot the shot that kills. It's partly about power, the hunt appeals a little to feelings of power. In the first place it's having power over the situation, that you control your own drives and yourself. At the same time there's something that [was] mentioned [in a video about prostitution]—that shooting a bear becomes a bigger exploit the longer you're hunted the bear.

The sexual conquest of the object, identifying and stalking the prey, the thrill of capture, degrading, ejaculating in, or killing the victim, and the orgiastic triumph over a defeated victim—with this narrative, one could be reading pornography, the testimony of a victim of sexual assault, a hunting story—or all three.

Hustler published a photograph captioned BEAVER HUNTERS. It featured two white men dressed as hunters sitting in a black Jeep, carrying

CHANG W. LEE / *NEW YORK TIMES*

rifles. A spread-eagled white woman is tied to the hood of the Jeep with thick rope.

In her book on *Pornography*, Andrea Dworkin describes the *Hustler* photograph:

Her head is turned to one side, tied down by rope that is pulled taut across her neck, extended to and wrapped several times around her wrists, tied around the rearview mirrors of the Jeep, brought back around her arms, crisscrossed under her breasts and over her thighs, drawn down and wrapped under the bumper of the Jeep, tied around her ankles. Between her feet on the car bumper, in orange with black print, is a sticker that reads: I brake for Billy Carter. The text under the photograph reads: "Western sportsmen report beaver hunting was particularly good through-out the Rocky Mountain region during the past season. These two hunters easily bagged their limit in the high country. They told Hustler *that they stuffed and mounted their trophy as soon as they got her home."*

The book *Wicked Words* helps us to register the slang meanings of words associated with *Beaver*.

Beaver which meant a "pelt" from a beaver, became slang for *beard*; and *beard*, already slang for women's pubic hair, passed that association along. It is also shorthand for *beaver hat*, and *hat* itself was another slang word for women's genitals. The animal known as beaver was known as *flat tail* and since *tail* meant *a woman considered as a sex object; a piece of tail* came to mean *the act of intercourse with the object*. (At first *tail* referred only to prostitutes, but by the twentieth century all women were included within the term.) Pornography gives us titles such as *Black Beaver Fever* and *Black Tail*.

The insertion of "Black" before these pornographic titles, Kimberlé Crenshaw points out, can galvanize an understanding of what harassment is:

While black women share with white women the experience of being objectified as "cunts," "beavers," or "pieces," for them those insults are many times prefaced with "black" or "nigger" or "jungle." Perhaps this racialization of sexual harassment explains why black women are disproportionately represented in sexual harassment cases. Racism may well provide the clarity to see that sexual harassment is neither a flattering gesture nor a misguided social overture but an act of intentional discrimination that is insulting, threatening, and debilitating.

Baseball player Jim Bouton tells us:

I better explain about beaver-shooting. A beaver-shooter is, at bottom, a Peeping Tom. It can be anything from peering over the top of the dugout to looking up dresses to hanging from the fire escape on the twentieth floor to look in a window. . . . Now some people might look down on this activity. But in baseball if you shoot a particularly good beaver you are . . . a folk hero of sorts.

Poor Beaver College! Although the college's name generated ridicule for its association with that innocent TV show *Leave It to Beaver*, it was probably doomed when *Hustler* began to encourage their readers to become pornographers themselves by sending in "beaver shots" of their sexual partners. Joked about by David Letterman, Conan O'Brien, and Howard Stern, and blocked by some search engines for teenagers, Beaver College finally conceded defeat and changed its name to Arcadia College.

Simone de Beauvoir, who explained just how it was that a woman is made, not born, was herself nicknamed "Beaver."

Men, too, are made, not born. The food writer for *GQ* magazine in the mid-1990s observed, "Boy food doesn't grow. It is hunted or killed." Perhaps that is why a Baltimore Burger King handed out coupons that read GOOD FOR

ONE FREE BOX OF AMMO WITH GUN PURCHASE OR 10 PERCENT OFF. A sign of effeminacy was not being able to kill. In a classic 1918 textbook on *War Neuroses*, John T. MacCurdy described a twenty-year-old private. Before the First World War, the private had exhibited "a tendency to abnormality in his make-up":

[He was] rather tender-hearted and never liked to see animals killed. Socially, he was rather self-conscious, inclined to keep to himself, and he had not been a perfectly normal, mischievous boy, but was rather more virtuous than his companions. He had always been shy with girls and had never thought of getting married.

As historian Joanna Bourke declares, "In other words, 'normal' men were psychologically capable of killing because they were tough, did not mind seeing animals killed, were gregarious and mischievous as youths, and were actively heterosexual."

This T-shirt was sold at a spring Block Party on Fraternity Row at Syracuse University in 1991. Though nearly 75 years intervened between the poor private who didn't want to kill and these T-shirts, the dominant view about heterosexual men is frighteningly consistent.

Men are not supposed to be interested in other men. They don't really care about seals, only about how to demean homosexuals.

Its assaultive nature arises, too, from the A/Not-A hierarchy: that protection would go to Not A's, like seals, over A's, humans, gay humans. It relies on anthropocentrism, human-centeredness, to convey its homophobia.

With hunting, bonds develop between men who hunt together, but they must have an outside target to justify their male bonding, otherwise their heterosexuality could be called

"Tables Turned"

into question. Besides conversing in a language that assumes women's object status, heterosexual hunters must devalue homosexual men to assure themselves that *they* aren't gay.

They bond together by having a shared victim.

During the 1990s, a pigeon shoot was held in Hegins, Pennsylvania. It involved releasing pigeons from cages, then competitors standing twenty yards away, would shoot at them as they were being released. Yearly, in front of an audience hostile to their viewpoint, protestors denounced the event. One seventh grader at Hegins wore a T-shirt that said, SAVE A PIGEON. KILL A PROTESTOR.

That same year, some protestors rushed onto the field with fake blood dripping from their mouths to try to free the caged birds. As state police tried to handcuff the activists, some spectators shouted "shoot." They also shouted obscenities and what the Associated Press politely called "homosexual slurs."

Male sexual power involves displaying power, including the power to degrade. By ritualizing the killing of Not-A's, men reaffirm their status as "A's."

Hunting, like pornography, also provides the compensation of dominance to those who themselves may be caught within the machinery of culture.

Most carnivores normally do not kill anything they are not going to be eating. They will not normally murder opponents of their same species (unless they are in captivity).

Carnivorous animals become the evil beasts of the animal kingdom.

Unlike wolves, humans can live on vegetable protein.

Unlike lions, humans kill merely to decorate their walls.

Unlike sharks, who kill out of hunger or self-defense, humans create institutions of captivity for those they wish to eat, cutting off the pigs' tails, severing chickens' beaks, and destroying bulls' genitals.

And when this ferocity of the armed hunter is pointed out, the human vegetarian must be tainted, too, for their vicious killing of plants. (Though it is meat eaters who actually are responsible for the mass destruction of plants—those that are fed to farmed animals, "protein factories in reverse" as Frances Moore Lappé famously called them. They must be fed six-to-twelve times the protein they will "produce.")

Just as humans displace the idea of their own cruelty, their own ferocity, their own bloodthirstiness, onto nonhumans—those fearsome, irresponsible, cruel beasts—so meat eaters wax poetic about the suffering of the carrot and the potato caused by a vegetarian.

Everyone is bloodthirsty except those humans who live on flesh.

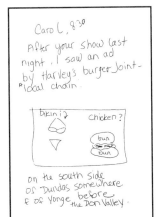

Carol, 8³⁰

After your show last
night, I saw an ad
by Harvey's burger Joint —
a local chain.

Bikini?   Chicken?

on the south side
of Dundas somewhere
E of Yonge   before
          the Don Valley.

9

Hookers

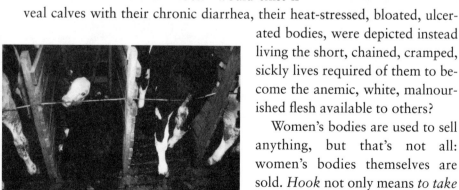

PROVIMI VEAL

Lean & Trim

THE HOOK IN ADVERTISING is what brings you into the ad. The hook is a *lure*, an enticement. It *catches* your attention. It promises something.

Women's bodies are often the "hook" in advertising.

The Provimi ad "hooks" with slim women, reinforcing the idea that women should be lean and trim. What sort of "hook" would exist if veal calves with their chronic diarrhea, their heat-stressed, bloated, ulcerated bodies, were depicted instead living the short, chained, cramped, sickly lives required of them to become the anemic, white, malnourished flesh available to others?

Women's bodies are used to sell anything, but that's not all: women's bodies themselves are sold. *Hook* not only means *to take strong hold of, to captivate*, it also means *to work as a prostitute*.

FARM

Bait is far from a natural category. As Joan Dunayer explains:

> *Animals used as live bait range from shrimps, lizards, worms, and frogs to mackerels, salmons, crickets, and crabs. "Bait-fish" are hooked so that they won't die quickly: through their lips, their nose, their eye sockets. . . . If large, they may be impaled on two or three hooks. Sometimes, to reduce drag, fishers sew a fish's mouth shut before towing them as bait. Because a fish who struggles and bleeds is especially likely to attract predators, fishers often break a "baitfish's" back, cut their fins, or notch them with multiple razor slits.*

Hooker, too, is far from a natural category. Women used as live bait, range from teenage girls (and younger), drug addicts living in a state of indentured servanthood, women kidnapped and sold into sexual slavery, women of color surviving in world regions where prostitution has overtaken entire populations of women—2 million in Thailand, 1 to 1.5 million in Korea, half a million in the Philippines.

According to the *American Heritage Dictionary*, *hooker* "portrays a prostitute who hooks, or snares, clients." How does such snaring transpire? These E-bay ads for "lures" show us.

Both of these advertised items are addressed simultaneously to men about women and to fishermen about catching fish: the lures attract "male fishes." The "Virgin Mermaid" we are told, "lures both men and fish. In

You are bidding on the HAWAIIAN "NAKED" HULA GIRL MERMAID DEEP SEA FISHING LURE. The lure is 101/2" long. She has a big STAR HOOK at her waist and a big DOUBLE HOOK below her feet. This lure also has a rubberize glittery hula skirt and painted flower lei on her neck. This is a totally new concept in fishing equipment. Never before has a DEEP SEA LURE be meant to attract only male fishes. This lure is painstakingly designed to catch the macho deep sea

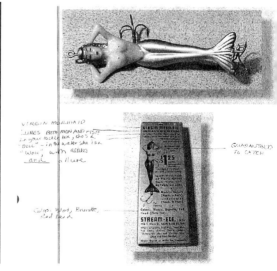

your tackle box, she's a 'doll'—in the water she is a 'wow' with action and allure. Guaranteed to catch."

The literal function of these lures is to hook a fish; usually the hook penetrates an area filled with nerves—the mouth, jaw, lip, or snout.

The idea that a sexualized woman's (or mermaid's) body will attract nonhuman animals would seem laughable if it weren't that so much of science that studies nonhuman animals has imposed similar sexist assumptions.

Females tempt with the promise of sex. They entice. They *lure*. Women who *bait* men not only are available, they want it.

Women need a hook (or do they need to hook?) to attract and "keep" men . . . keep them happy, keep them sexually turned on, keep their attention from straying.

Three stages, like a three-ring circus, with bodies on display for entertainment. Three stages, yes, but three stages ALL NUDE. The girls must drop their fishnets.

Advertisements in the general culture never let us forget that a woman's

worth is determined by her appeal to men. Her thoughts, feelings, experiences—these don't matter as much as having the right panties or knowing when to drop those "fishnets." She is an object to be judged, evaluated, and deemed desirable by the observer. She exists to be a sexed body.

Whore. Hooker. The key to understanding these words and their many synonyms is that they are the vocabulary by which men might speak of any woman. They may be *sluts,* who do it with or without being paid, or expensive *courtesans*—either way, they are viewed as available, whether *at a price* or not.

When men go to prostitutes they often want to try out "ideas" they have gotten from pornography.

Prostituted women have to dissemble involvement and interest in men.

How to inflame his ardor? Serve the man beef, says the author, who has been happily married for 40 years. From New Woman, *1996*

Their "luring" is within a framework that men need to believe they are being lured, that the object wants to be an object. Kathy Barry explains that sex in prostitution involves "Distancing oneself in order to become disembodied and then acting as if the experience is embodied." The result is that "Men buy not a self but a body that performs as a self."

Like pornography, the message of culture is that all women should perform for their man, to keep him "caught." As with the "live bait"—some with broken backs—they are there because someone has created them as something.

What do men want? asks the happily-married-for-forty-years author of "Love, Sex and Flank Steak."

Answer:

Great sex and a great steak and not necessarily in that order. Sure, they want money and power, but only because of what those can win them— sex and steak. Both are closely related, as muscular, full-bodied pleasures of the flesh, and each ignites desire for the other. A hot, juicy, blood-red steak or a succulently thick hamburger induces an overall sense of well-being and a surge of self-assurance that is sure to make him feel good about himself and by association, you. That is especially true in this country, where beef is the quintessential macho fare.

actual heading ↓

man-pleasing brunch

for actual recipe, from Cosmopolitan mag. ↓

(don't ask what i was doing with a Cosmo)

A recipe for a man-pleasing brunch from *Cosmopolitan* required potatoes and four cups of beef. "Don't ask what I was doing with a *Cosmo*," my young correspondent wrote.

Well what was she doing? Learning how to hook a man?

The veggie burger ad promises *You won't lose your husband if you become a vegetarian. Yes, we know they want sex and steak . . . but here's a way to keep them happy.*

Whose are the words of *"Come hungry"*? A slut, a vamp, a hooker, a wife, a tease . . . or a waitress?

A restaurant called Pig Pickins featured women waiting tables with T-shirts that said TENDER AND JUICY FOR YOU.

Female servers at Hooters used to have to wear T-shirts that said, MORE THAN A MOUTHFUL.

Half the fun of our veggie burger is eating. The other half, tricking your husband.

It's a thrill, pulling the burger switch-a-roo on an unsuspecting family. Who can blame you? What they want to eat and what they're supposed to are rarely one in the same. We're out to change that. At Morningstar Farms, we make the foods you love meat-free. Breakfast Links, Chik Nuggets, Corn Dogs for the kids. And America's Original Veggie Burgers. Made from wholesome grains and vegetable protein. They're one part healthy. One part fun. And altogether delicious. Look for them in your grocer's freezer if they're not already in your own.

Morningstar Farms. Enjoy eating better.

Which is a bigger surprise: how good they are, or how good they are for you?

Veggie burgers, hot dogs & more. Grill 'em. Serve 'em. Watch 'em disappear.

MORNINGSTAR Grillers

A teaser, according to my *Dictionary of American Slang,* is *A girl or woman who seems to invite a male's attention and favors, but who does not return them when given; a cock teaser.* She lures, she baits, but she does not deliver.

A strip tease involves a performer slowly removing clothing, usually to music, until she (usually a she), stands on stage, ALL NUDE.

DOUGLAS BUCHANAN

Strip tease?

Women want you to want them.

Women are both the hook *and* a hooker.

What do men want?

The advertisers, the writers for women's magazines, and pornographers provide the same answer: Sex and steak . . . and not necessarily in that order.

How is such tension resolved? A *hook* that promises them both: strip tease.

Come hungry indeed.

10

The Fish in Water Problem

G. **MAIN DISH TOWELS.** Beef, pork and fish—potted up and ready for cooking—on our 27x17″ cotton tea towels. Or, perhaps each tasty beast is just contemplating the future . . . Cow, A-09548. Pig. A-09696. Fish, A-09571. Each **$5.00**; 2 for **$9.00**.

CALL TOLL-FREE 800-228-5656
24 HOURS—7 DAYS
(In Nebraska, Call 800-642-8777)

M ARSHALL MCLUHAN ONCE NOTED, "if a fish could speak, water is the last thing it would identify as part of its environment."

Catharine MacKinnon observes, "All women live in sexual objectification the way fish live in water."

And so do nonhumans when they stand in for women.

Mrs. Claus's Sexy Santa Suit!
How does Mrs. Claus spend her Christmas Eve? Waiting to surprise Santa! Whimsically wicked in its front-and-back silkscreening, designer Chris Zoch's eye-catching Santa suit adds a bit of spice to winter getaways. Great as a nightshirt, too! 50% cotton/50% poly. Hand washable. Made in USA. *Color:* White. One size fits most; 30″ long.
V25-801 Mrs. Claus's Santa Suit **$29.95**

Back

TITIAN, *VENUS OF URBINO*

The *Venus of Urbino* is one of the most familiar images in Western art. By the middle of the twentieth century, when this pig was posed in imitation, it had become a commonplace to interpret the *Venus of Urbino* (rightly or wrongly) as a painting whose model was a prostitute.

Note the dog asleep on Venus's bed. Recall that one aspect of pornography is to install a nonhuman animal in the scene to suggest the animalizing of the woman. (Recall, too, the words of the woman from the "Club": "one even brought me a puppy.")

The question has to be asked of both of them: Are they masturbating? Those who manipulated the pig offer the answer that at first art historians hesitated to admit about Venus: her genitalia are not being *covered*, they are being *stimulated*.

The major difference between them is the gaze: Venus beholds us directly, but would, or could, the pig?

Is the pig alive or dead?

And in between them, a pose from the fashion section of the *New York Times* magazine. Dressed in pink, bathed in phallic symbols, she refers back to Venus and forward to the pig.

What do you see in the pose of the pig? Her painted toenails? The bikini panties? Her trotter tucked into her panties like a hand? Her smooth legs? Her facial expression beaming pleasure, relaxation, entice-ment, desire? Her notched ear to show ownership?

Is that the kind of drink that hides the drugs of a date rapist? Is that why she looks passed out? If she were in some fraternities, her unconscious state would be seen as "asking for it."

Next to the drink, sits a cat lamp (the *suggestion* of another animal). But look more quickly at the cat's leg and foot. Are they shaped to recall a black dildo?

The luxury implied in this photograph is important too. Is this perhaps modeled after a Victorian brothel?

With this masturbating pig, we encounter the scene setting of pornography. All the cues are there so that this is a pornographic shot. Pornography sends these cues that this is sex. That we can look at a pig and know that this is pornography is because of these cues. The images here are ways to convey the message, "I can't be wealthy, but I can own a woman. I can eat meat."

Of the late designer Gianni Versace, Richard Martin, the curator of the Costume Institute at the Metropoli-tan Museum of Art, said, "He looked at prostitute style and made it high style in the eighties." When I present my slide show, I ask for a male volunteer to come for-ward when this slide of a Versace dress is projected on the screen. I ask him to face the audience and invite them to tell him how to pose so that he imitates this Versace ad. There is some laughter.

Then, a voice, usually female, calls out: "Stick your butt out." Other voices join in, both male and female: "Show your breasts." "Take off your shirt." "Put your hand on your crotch." "Balance on your toes." "Suck in your cheeks." "Look dead."

More laughter occurs, as the man attempts to conform his body to these commands. We applaud him for trying and I ask him how he felt. "Uncomfortable." "Weird." "Awkward." "I don't know how women do it."

I point out that those men are not used to "swimming in women's wa-ter." One young man, who had a hidden life dressing in drag, most closely approximated this pose with ease.

Versace's "high prostitute style" of clothing is a reminder that women are socialized to act *and* dress like whores.

Posing a man makes the water that is sexual objectification visible, if only briefly. The directions that are called out to the man, like the posing of a pig in a pornographic scenario, highlight what I call cues of violability.

Cues of violability are cues of inequality. Women learn to exhibit, rather than to inhabit their bodies. These cues arise through three main arenas: *appearance*, *gestures*, and *ornamentation*.

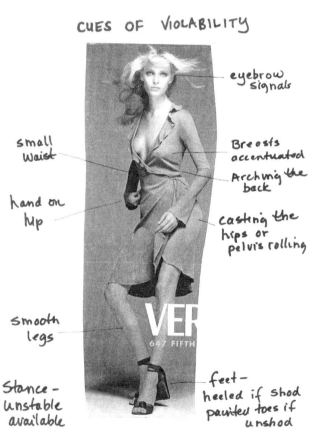

CUES OF VIOLABILITY

eyebrow signals

small waist

Breosts accentuated

Arching the back

hand on hip

casting the hips or pelvis rolling

smooth legs

Stance - unstable available

feet - heeled if shod painted toes if unshod

Configuration/appearance:

- Small waist.
- Accentuated breasts.
- Smooth legs
- Eyelashes curled (like the pig's in *Hamtastic*)

Gestures/postures/movement:

- Casting the hips or pelvis rolling
- Arching the back
- An exposed and unstable stance that telegraphs, "I cannot hold my ground."
- Arm signals
- Eyebrow signals

Ornamentation:

- Garter and bra—a fetish of underclothes
- Earrings
- Bracelets
- Heels or painted toes (like the painted toenails of the "Venus" pig).

These cues show how inequality is made sexy. Take Betty Boop, for instance. Betty Boop was originally drawn as a feminine, "voluptuous," little dog with long ears. Soon earrings replaced the long ears, and she became a cute "girl." Just like Betty's transformation from dog to girl, cues of violability are taken from the Not-A side of the dualism and include as well rear-end views, nakedness, the presence or suggestion of an animal, and the fetish of skin color.

Cues of violability themselves are fragmented body parts, in which the accentuated body part stands for the whole, available, "fuckable" woman. ("I'm here; come and get me.") Cues of violability for women are the basic scene setting of pornography: she desires penetration.

In chapter 2, I proposed that nonhuman animals become absent referents through the institution of meat eating. Through socialization to sexual objectification, women become absent referents as well.

Absent referent formula
Woman + cues of violability =
sexy/sexualized dominance/inequality made sexy/
destruction of subject status.

Just as with the structure of the absent referent in meat eating, another being can replace "woman" and the fact of sexualized dominance will still be present—as long as the someone taking the woman's place is also from the Not-A side of the dualism. Otherwise it is a mere parody.

The substitution makes the sexualizing culture of which we are a part visible because the taken-for-grantedness of women's bodies is replaced by the surprise that other animals are being pornographed. Just as the normalized act of butchering assumed horrific qualities when used against a woman in the example of the *Hustler* cover, so the depiction of woman as sex object becomes explicitly a construct and, in that, a forced identity when imposed upon another Not-A being, like a pig.

The absent referent is a woman. To make the nonhuman violable, we make those animals "female." Cues of violability construct female consumability. Consider the turkey hooker on the next page.

Here are all the cues of violability: "Here I am. I am available." The farmed animal becomes a stand in for a woman. What is absent is "woman."

What do the pose of the turkey and the pose in the Versace ad share in common? Both are the pose of a hooker . . . a purchasable commodity. And just in case we missed all the visual references, they are repeated through words: *an easy pick up* from pan to platter. Here the phallic symbol of the snake/penis/asparagus is replaced by a hook.

Is the hooker the paradigmatic consumable female? An interesting study of prostitution in Norway, *Backsteets,* found that "The number of peepers is much higher than the number of customers. This means that far more men than just the customers have a concrete, visual relation to prostitution: it becomes images on the retina that can flash by in situations and places far removed from prostitution."

Like the turkey-filled oven on Thanksgiving?

Prostitution, they conclude, *is about men's sexuality*. And pornography means *writing about whores, writing about hookers*. So pornography, too, is about men's sexuality.

These depictions of a pig or a turkey are not just anthropomorphic images. They too are about men's sexuality—with a twist. They are *anthropornography*.

11

Anthropornography

ANTHROPORNOGRAPHY IS THE depiction of nonhuman animals as whores.

Imagine opening the lifestyle section of your local paper. Imagine it is the *Seattle Post-Intelligencer* of March 29, 2000. The headline A REAL CHEAP DISH grabs you immediately. These words, occupying a six-by-five-inch center of the page, dwarf all other text there. These words command: LOOK HERE.

And right there, with her rump hanging way over a champagne glass, is, what else? A real dish—with one high heel pump kicked off, the other about ready to fall, her pink fishnet stockings pulled thigh-high. She has big pink lips, mascara-ed eyes, and a large feather standing erect at the top of her head.

Clad in a very skimpy bikini, she thrusts toward you, thrusts toward the words, A REAL CHEAP DISH. Her rump and the word *real* appear to be responding to each other. But she is not just your ordinary sex object. Unlike strippers of old who might have had the words *US Navy* tattooed upon a heart in some tempting place, *her* tattoo says USDA on top of a blue heart.

Nine-and-half-inches high

(bigger than this book!) she rises above the words a REAL CHEAP DISH, showing us all just who is a real cheap dish—a cow. Her body is for you. And the article that is dwarfed by the headline and this posed, sexually attractive "come-and-get-me-big-boy" cow is about fixing cheap cuts of meat.

With anthropornography the attitudes toward women found in *Playboy* and other heterosexual pornography can be expressed freely yet in a disguised way—with nonhuman animals as the objects.

In its positioning of nonhumans as sex objects, anthropornography throws what pornography does into relief: pornography reproduces inequality.

With anthropornography the inequality of species conveys the inequality of gender. When imposed on a nonhuman, we see that gender is not *difference* but *dominance*. What appears to be a feature of life is actually a one-sided construct. The point of view of the entire culture, reiterated through advertisements, newspaper illustrations, a melding of pornography and popular culture, is actually only a particular point of view.

This point of view, refined and enacted by looking, creates the condition

for *someone* to become *something*.

Like a curtain, a striptease act covers what is supposed to be hidden so that it can uncover what is supposed to be seen.

Anthropornography gives you a hooker on your plate. Nonhuman animals are whoring for you. Nonhumans want you, too. Suffering? Slaughtering? Inhumane acts? No. They *want* it. That is what the ads want you to believe. Yet, farmed-animals' lives are barren and filled with daily cruelties. The idea that they would desire their own exploitation—why it is like the lie that girls desire sexual abuse. Speaking of which, consider *Playboar.*

Clearly, the *Playboar* image is based on the image from Stanley Kubrick's *Lolita* of the 1960s. For censorship reasons, Kubrick could not present the idea of "nymphets" that is so central to Nabokov's book. In fact, it is Nabokov who coined the term, drawing together the idea of *nymph* as a synonym for *pupa* (insect nymphs resemble adults except they are smaller); nymph as *spritelike deities,* and nymph, the Greek root word that is at the base of *nymphomania,* a male-defined word about women ("excessive sexual desire in and behavior by a female"). There is a similar word for men *(satyriasis)* but the fact that most people aren't familiar with it says worlds about sexual behavior: men never have too much of it.

Nymphet: a *pubescent girl regarded as sexually desirable.* Regarded by whom?

A partial view, *the viewpoint of someone who sees women or young girls as sex objects,* becomes total.

The exact connection between Nabokov's role as a lepidopterist, a butterfly cataloguer, and his descriptions of Humbert Humbert's passion for Lolita is debated: whether the hunt for a specific kind of butterfly has been nuanced into the hunt for a specific kind of female.

What is not arguable is that after the publication of Nabokov's novel, the nymphet Lolita gave her name not only to a new species of butterfly, but also to a widely traded pornographic magazine and to an entire genre of pornography.

Descriptions of pornographic films telegraph their content in statements such as:

- 14-year-old Lolita schoolgirl is drawn into a web of vice, including bondage and whipping. A must for Lolita fans.
- Sweet 10-year-old Lolita does not feel well and goes to the doctor . . . it does not take him long to get into her pussy. . . .

- *Lolitas Who Love Pissing* dedicated to depicting groups of men and boys urinating on a little girl.

Nymphs in mythology were often pursued and raped by more powerful deities. Child pornography documents the rape and sexual abuse of children by more powerful deities, their parents, relatives and friends. (Only fifteen percent of children are molested by strangers.) Individual pedophiles record themselves abusing children. They then barter, exchange, or sell them to other abusers.

When a sexual abuser targets a child, he too engages in grooming behavior. He might begin by having the child sit on his lap, or look at a book or magazine with him. When the content of the material they look at together is child sexual abuse, the goal becomes to lower the inhibitions of the targeted child. Such material may be used to persuade younger children to try sexual acts because they will enjoy them. ("See how happy those children in the picture look?")

Pornography may also be used in the hope of arousing older children. Whether for young or old, the material chosen aims to persuade them that what they are being asked to do is acceptable, OK, fun. Child abusers may also use child pornography to arouse themselves before abusing a child. Men sexually interested in children use pornographic books and films to validate their sexual feelings. The child is the "tease": she's *Kneeling for Daddy.* When she's not *Daddy's Naughty Daughter*, she is *Daddy's Hot Daughter*, or perhaps, she is one of the many *Daughters Hot for Dogs.*

"Of course, if your taste is for pig-meat, he begs us to pity his daughter." This reference, from Aristophanes' *The Wasps*, arises from a pun in the Greek: *choiros* meant both *pig* and "female genitalia."

Daughters need more than our pity. One-half of all rape victims are under eighteen years of age; twenty-five percent of rape victims are under twelve years of age. The youngest known victim of sexual abuse was one-week old.

A pimp explained to Richard Kluft what he looks for in a woman he is considering to make into one of his prostitutes:

Beauty, yes. Sexual expertise, somewhat. That can be taught easier than you think. What is important above all is obedience. And how do you get obedience? You get obedience if you get women who have had sex with their fathers, their uncles, their brothers—you know, someone they love and fear to lose so that they do not dare to defy. Then you are nicer to the woman than they ever were, and more dangerous as well.

Fifteen to fifteen and a half. This is the average age that a woman begins working in prostitution (according to surveys from places as diverse as Vancouver and Norway).

Mainstream pornography finds numerous ways to sexualize age hierarchies. Cartoons and illustrations may depict children, children who "want" it. For instance, a *Playboy* cartoon presents a child as the seductress of a middle-aged man asking, "You call that being molested?" *Hustler* magazine featured a cartoon character "Chester the Molester," who sexually stalked girls.

The prepubescent girl is associated not just with youthfulness, but with vulnerability, powerlessness, and virginity. When adult women are shown with shaved pubic regions, youthfulness is sexualized. Shaved pubic regions, like the enforced shaving of heads, deprive one of one's individuality. *Baby Dolls* shows women (over eighteen we are assured) with shaved pubic regions, blurring women with children and with one another.

A further way that children are introduced into mainstream pornography is by running a photo of the "Playmate" as a child. Placing it in this sexual context, and using double entendres, (for example a photo of a two-year-old girl with the question "What's your next trick?"), keeps the pornographic use of the *Lolita* myth alive.

What does all this have to do with the nymphet on page 110, the *Playboar* cover pig? Is *Playboar* a publication for those who have fixated on nonhuman animals as the exclusive focus of their sexual desires, those who call themselves *zoophiles?* The zoophile's worldview is similar to the rapist's and child sexual abuser's. They all view the sex they have with their victims as consensual, and they believe it benefits their sexual "partners" as well as themselves. Just as pedophiles differentiate between those who abuse children and those who love children—placing themselves, of course, in the latter group—zoophiles distinguish between animal sexual abusers (bestialists) and those who love animals (zoophiles). In each of these cases, these distinctions are only self-justifications.

No, *Playboar* is seeking a more mainstream audience than the zoophile. (Notice the subtle reference to football on the cover—"Pigskin.") *Playboar* suggests that nonhuman animals are not only like *whores*, but like *nymphets*, curious, eager, preternaturally sexual.

Pigs *need* it.

But apparently they actually don't. Recently, a Belgian company developed a vibrator for pigs. Why? Because *the hardest part is getting in.* So a vibrator has been created to sexually stimulate the pig and make it "easier" for sows to undergo artificial insemination. The vibrator is connected with a tube to a syringe containing sperm from the boar. If the pig is aroused, the sperm from the boar supposedly will glide more easily into her uterus.

To paraphrase Jean-Jacques Rousseau, everywhere nonhuman animals are in chains but we image them as free. Not simply as free, though they are not, but as sexually free. Simultaneously, these images confirm that women aren't only free, but sexually free. This denial, then, works on two levels—we aren't doing what we are doing to animals, and of course we aren't doing it to women, either.

To make a great pâté, you have to be pig-headed.

Trois Petits Cochons
three little pigs ™
All natural pâtés.
Live like pigs.
AVAILABLE WHEREVER
DISCRIMINATING TASTE PREVAILS

Because of breeding for select traits of rapid growth and leanness, pigs develop weak bones but large muscles. They are now more fragile and likely to die during transport. Are producers pushing animals beyond their biological limits? Yes, according to livestock-insurance companies that will not sell transport insurance to producers to cover these pigs.

Although vegetarians, vegans, and animal activists are accused of anthropomorphizing animals—of projecting human qualities onto nonhuman animals—it seems that really it is meat eaters and anthropornographers who do this.

Animal activists know that animals are like human beings because human beings *are* animals.

Meat eaters, meat advertisers, and anthropornographers take the dangerous knowledge of our similarity to nonhuman animals and sexualize it.

CAROL J. ADAMS

Consider this painting on the side of Razoos, a Cajun restaurant chain.

Ask yourself, Who are the predators here? Perhaps it is the leering male crayfish ogling the large-breasted bikini-ed crayfish. Or is the predator the toothy alligator? Certainly the white male is not the predator. His is the most innocent image, with a Little League hat, and he's got a heart.

Razoos creates the feeling of innocence for the true consumers here. It presents the dominant point of view back to those who benefit from it by saying, *We aren't visually consuming women (and heavens, certainly not girls!). These are just animals.*

Anthropornography provides a way for men to bond publicly around misogyny. Men can publicly consume what is usually private. Razoos, like *Playboar,* assures its consumers that everything is OK, their worldview is OK. It makes the degradation and consumption of women's images and of meat appear playful and harmless, "just a joke." Because women are not being depicted, no one is seen as being harmed and so no one has to be accountable. Everyone can enjoy the degradation of women without being honest about it.

"We're just looking at a pig."

"We're just eating at Razoos, Common Grounds, Hooters. . . ."

Everyone knows that at one level they aren't talking about owls or pigs. But why the continual need to shore up the nature not just of humanness, but, specifically, of human maleness, at the expense of recognizing our relationship with nonhuman animals?

To recognize connections would mean feeling sympathy for another being. This requires acknowledging the privileged position one occupies in the world, the privilege created by inequality.

12

I Ate a Pig

*O*INK, OINK, OINK, a group of high school athletes would say when any young woman came into view whom they viewed as a potential sex toy. Their parties—*PIG-nics*— required the girls to call themselves "pigs" to be admitted.

Later, the athletes were charged with raping a retarded seventeen-year-old with a broomstick and baseball bat. When, in the presence of thirteen male students, the broomstick was rammed into her vagina, one of the young men called her *Pigorskia.*

Michael Querques, a lawyer for one of the athletes, provided this description of the young woman whose IQ was that of an eight-year old:

This girl is a pig . . . She's just a plain pig. If she wasn't retarded, everybody'd say, She's a pig. She's somebody I'd keep my kids away from. I'd make sure I protected them from her.

MEGAN HAGLER

The all-male club members of Pi Eta, whose members are Harvard undergraduates and graduates, received a letter in the 1980s that promised "a bevy of slobbering bovines fresh for the slaughter" at their parties. As Peggy Sanday explains, the logic of such parties (at which women are frequently raped, including at this fraternity) is "Its male participants brag about their masculinity and its female participants are degraded to the status of what the boys call 'red meat' or 'fish.'"

Members of a fraternity in which fraternity members had raped an unconscious woman referred to it as a *corpse riff.*

A T-shirt spied in 2001: 10,000 BATTERED WOMEN AND I'M STILL EATING MINE *PLAIN?!*

In the 1937 Rape of Nanking, in which between 260,000 to 350,000 people were killed and 20,000 to 80,000 women were raped, many soldiers, after raping the women, sliced off their breasts, disemboweled them, or nailed them alive to walls. "Perhaps when we were raping her, we looked at her as a woman," one soldier rationalized, "but when we killed her, we just thought of her as something like a pig."

According to the *Dictionary of American Slang*, a pig is *a promiscuous woman, especially one who is blousy and unattractive.*

Over the past twenty years or so, a frightening number of prostitutes in Vancouver have been disappearing. Families and friends insisted to the police that someone was stalking prostitutes. People in Vancouver wondered if Seattle's elusive "Green River Killer," blamed for the death or disappearance of forty-nine women—mostly prostitutes or runaways—had moved his efforts north.

The majority of missing women got their start as child prostitutes. A survey of women working as prostitutes in Vancouver's Downtown Eastside area in 1995, found that 73 percent of them had started as children. One area of Vancouver was known to have a "kiddie stroll" where girls, some as young as eleven, worked on the street. Three-quarters were aboriginal. (In Canada, aboriginal women between the ages of 25 and 44 are five times more likely to experience a violent death than other women of that same-age group.)

A few years ago, a lead was provided: a woman had escaped from a man who had come after her with a knife. He lived on a pig farm. The farm, once isolated, was now gaining neighbors—urban development of nearby land for single-family housing for Vancouver's middle class. For some reason, this lead never actually came to anything. More women disappeared.

Over the years, the pig-farmer brothers raised fewer pigs, instead selling fill-dirt and gravel from the farm and dabbling in building demolition. The farm became a site for the staging of late-night parties and pig roasts. Women working as prostitutes were hired and brought in from nearby Vancouver to work in the makeshift, unlicensed nightclub known as Piggy's Palace.

The disappearance of more than one hundred women had been largely ignored in the media. But then the police put this pig farm under lock and key, searching for the bodies of the missing women. Soon speculation began as to what exactly the nature of the "pig" meat was that this farm had been selling. Now, the owner of the pig farm has been charged with the murder of some of the women.

Watch the movement of meaning in this definition of *pig*: *A girl or woman having a sloppy appearance; a girl or woman with "sloppy" morals; a passionate or promiscuous woman; any girl or woman.* "Common, esp. among male students." The definition begins with comments on women's appearance (remember "blousy"!), then, by association, with "morals" (or lack thereof), and finally it applies to all women.

Explaining the care with which they were approaching the explosive story breaking in Vancouver, the news director for British Columbia TV issued a dictum that no one was to refer to the missing women as "hookers." He clarified, "We wanted to ensure they were treated as women." His comment acknowledges the cultural dualism of good women/bad, "dirty" whore. But such a dualistic construction is truly nonexistent, at least from the viewpoint of women: when the Yorkshire "Ripper" was stalking and killing women (mainly prostitutes) in the north of England in the 1970s, many women called in to report that their husbands or lovers might be possible suspects.

Prostitution provides the male consumer with a class of people he needs—anonymous, throwaway, dehumanized women, whose disappearance is unnoticed. We do not even know how many prostitutes are murdered, dismembered, disemboweled, by their pimps or their "customers."

The repetition of the stories of prostitute murders including the fixation on Jack the Ripper occurs not because it is the working out of the trauma of women's deaths, but because it provides a sexualized script about women's corpses.

Like batterers who leave the newspaper open to a report on a woman's death at the hands of her husband, with the unspoken reminder that "This could be you . . . ," salacious reporting on women's murders, especially the murder of prostitutes, also provides a warning. "Stay indoors! You need protection!"

The knife is a popular implement in the pornographic script: women are shown mutilating their own genitals; a smiling young woman is shown thrusting a large butcher knife into her vagina, blood spurting from her wounds.

Vagina is the Latin for *sheath*. A *sheath* is a *case for a blade*. In pornography, women's sheaths receive not only knives, but daggers, razors, scissors, swords, hooks, jackhammers, axes, icepicks, cigarettes, needles, pokers.

So what is the purpose of the knives in these advertisements?

It takes a *knife* to eat meat, to butcher animals. The knife separates meat eaters from vegetarians; it horrifies vegetarians (supposedly) because it reminds them of the butchering that motivates the entire structure. But isolated from the act of butchering, it stands erect, reassuring, a commanding Freudian-phallic symbol, announcing triumph.

The knife actually expresses hostility to vegetarians. Who do these vegetarians think they are?

This not-very-subtle hostility to women and vegetarians (Are they actually two different groups in their eyes?) receives further male support with the billboard that tells vegetarians to eat the bun.

Just to be sure that we get the message, the phallic symbol—the hot dog—is erect as well.

I ate a pig. The male bravado of that statement proclaims, *I wouldn't not eat a pig, I wouldn't be a vegetarian*: the male right to eat meat is proclaimed, whether through blatant T-shirt or assertive knife.

With John Thomas's establishment we have several reminders of the accessibility of women's bodies to men. First, of course, is the double entendre for the word *strip*. Then, the knife as a phallic symbol represents all those John Thomases who want a piece. (John Thomas, famously the slang for penis in D. H. Lawrence's *Lady Chatterley's Lover*.)

Ninety percent of serial murders take place against women and girls.

Speaking of threatening behavior:

Ithaca's Only Prime Strip Joint.

"..John Thomas, one need only compare with a few famous steakhouses: Smith and Wollensky or the Post House in Manhattan, Morton's both in Chicago and Boston,.."

JOHN THOMAS
STEAKHOUSE
(607) 273-3464

Dinner starts at 5:30 every day

1152 DANBY ROAD • ITHACA, NY 14850

VEGETARIANS CAN EAT THE BUN.

Wienerschnitzel

Horrifying Vegetarians Since 1980.

The Post House
New York City

I had always been fond of her in the most innocent, asexual way. It was as if her body was always entirely hidden behind her radiant mind, the modesty of her behavior, and her taste in dress. She had never offered me the slightest chink through which to view the glow of her nakedness. And now suddenly the butcher knife of fear had slit her open. She was an open to me as the carcass of a heifer slit down the middle and hanging on a hook. There we were . . and suddenly I felt a violent desire to make love to her. Or to be more exact, a violent desire to rape her.

from Milan Kundera, The Book of Laughter and Forgetting

In sexual murder, a woman's corpse is "written" upon through dismemberment, disemboweling, continual knife penetrations, or the slashing off of her breasts or genitals.

In advertisements, the woman's body is an erotic screen to deflect yet celebrate the violence of meat eating. A sexual murderer treats a corpse like a carcass. An anthropornographer treats what is called a *carcass* (the body of a nonhuman) as female.

A recent book on children's relationship with animals, *Why the Wild Things Are*, suggests that children see nonhuman animals as their peers. A peer is your equal. A peer is your friend. Unless stranded and starving and in the presence of dead companions, one does not eat one's peers. (Though human flesh tastes "remarkably like beef" report people who have had to feed on their traveling companions.)

If children see animals as their peers, eating them would be a form of cannibalism. Is this the lingering message of the anthropornographed form? Bernard Shaw called meat eating "cannibalism with the heroic dish removed." Do meat advertisers reinsert the heroic dish through anthropornography?

Just as anything can be sex (for instance, in *Portnoy's Complaint*, when Portnoy masturbates in a piece of liver he bought at a butcher shop), so murder is sex for those who make it sex.

Recall psychotherapist Ellyn Kaschak's understanding of the oedipal complex, as a male entitlement that subsumes others, especially females, who are experienced as extensions of the man himself. Kaschak proposes that one aspect of the unresolved oedipal complex is the flight from death. She sees this manifested when men replace the aging bodies of their wives with the young and desirable bodies of daughters (literally daughters through incest and figuratively daughters through the acquisition of "trophy wives").

Why this flight from death, though? The body is material and will decay, and die. Although this could be seen as a good, as part of a continuum, as a return to nature, this is not the prevailing viewpoint. Since we are alienated from nature, death is seen oppositionally, as an extinction. And it is women, Eve or Pandora for example, who are blamed for bringing death into the world. (In fact, as mothers they bring life into the world.)

Why this confusion about women's role in life and death?

Though we actually don't know whether nonhumans are symbol makers—dolphins, for one, appear to display modes of communication that we barely comprehend—the assumption is that human beings are the symbol makers of the animal kingdom. Erich Fromm put it this way, "human beings are half-animal and half-symbolic."

In fact, it is men who have had the power of representation; women have been the objects of representation. As Gerda Lerner says: "Man (male) has found a way of dealing with this existential dilemma [that the body is material and will decay and die] by assigning symbol-making power to himself and life-death-nature finiteness to woman."

Consider the first creation myth to appear in written form, a story of matricide, sometimes called the "Babylonian Genesis." In a rebellion against the mother by her male children, Marduk slays the Great Goddess Tiamat. Her body parts are then used to create the universe. Marduk splits Tiamat's corpse into two parts, "like a bi-valved shellfish," which become heaven and earth. Her buttocks became the mountains; her breasts, the foothills.

Marduk's fate? He who killed Tiamat was not only the hero, he became God.

So a sexual murderer "becomes God" and is able to claim himself not a destroyer, but a creator.

Butchering of women becomes the primordial act of the hero and the representation of sexual murder helps to constitute, or reconstitute, a social identity, a male identity.

A basic issue with women's deaths in art/film/popular culture/pornography is that we are always supposed to see beyond it to something else, something evoked, something metaphoric, something more powerful and important than the woman's body—*an idea.*

Scholars have explored what the dead woman's body represents: sex, body, carnality, dirt/filth, earth, and the rejection of nature in earth and in death. The fixation on a woman's corpse is a way for men to feel transcendence. Diana York Blaine explains, "By visualizing death as a woman, male painters and authors could fantasize their own transcendence of this state; as long as they were not women, they were not bodies, and it is bodies that die."

To transcend the material, the bodily, means overcoming or breaking away from that which is defined as feminine.

According to Kaschak, for men to resolve their oedipal conflict with its expansive boundaries over women, they have to want to move beyond that stage. To do this, they have to forego the pleasure they receive from women as objects. Instead, it is Jocasta who dies; the mother/wife who was passed like property from king to king. Bahama Mama gives the unresolved oedipal complex of men an added twist.

Women used in meat advertisements aren't selling a product through "sex appeal." Women are being used to re-present sexual murders, of which meat eating just may be one facet. To understand fully what I mean we have to consider why batterers harm non-humans.

Many ways exist to say "I want you dead." One way is to kill the person. Another is to kill something associated with that person.

Batterers know what they are doing, to whom they are doing it, and what it is that they are doing. Abusive men are the major source of injury to adult women in the United States. The World Health Organization, in the first comprehensive documentation of global violence released in October, 2002, found that forty to seventy percent of female murder victims in Australia, the United States, Canada, Israel, and South Africa were killed by their husbands or boyfriends.

How many batterers also kill nonhumans in their household is less documented. But it is clear that many women realized that their partners were planning to kill them when they killed a dog, a cat, a horse.

In documented cases, batterers have slashed cats to death; ordered a dog to sit still and then shot him; hunted down kittens and picked them off, one by one with a gun; stepped on and killed a dachshund; killed the sheep his partner was caring for.

A batterer will demonstrate "omnipotence" to suggest the futility of resistance, to prove his power, to teach submission. Killing a nonhuman is an example of such omnipotence. One man forced his wife to watch him dig her grave, kill the family cat, and decapitate a pet horse. Making someone watch the torture of another is ultimate mastery, saying through these actions, "This is what I can do and there is nothing you can do to stop me." She may wish to protect the animal, but she realizes she is unable to.

Before Vronksy kills his human mistress in *Anna Karenina*, he breaks the back of his mare.

Batterers do not want people to know how purposeful, willful, and deliberate their actions are. Batterers can obfuscate why they batter when it is physical violence (claiming "I lost control and punched her") and they can confuse the issue of sexual assault (asserting "she was teasing me and said she wanted it"). But loss of control in a relationship with an animal is harder to defend because the deliberateness of the violence is exposed in the description, ("I 'lost' control and then cut the dog's head off and then nailed it to the porch.")

After I spoke on her campus, a woman told me of her experience:

I had a boyfriend who was and remains a hog farmer. He named one of his hogs "Cathie" after me. He wanted to get married, have children, the

whole nine yards. I didn't want to. He named his pig Cathie because she wouldn't breed. He beat me—not more than a couple of times because I left. He warned me that he would kill me if I ever left him.

After I broke up with him, he came to my parents' home and gave them a gift—sausage that he had made from "Cathie."

It is true, as the T-shirt claims: HE ATE A PIG. Now we understand what that really means.

13

Average White Girl

ROWS OF DEAD, EVISCERATED PIGS hang in a meat locker. Their legs are parted so that a special clamp can hold them, hanging downward from the ceiling. They are clearly dead pigs: one nearest our sight is beheaded and the front legs appear amputated; this pig has no innards. They are all dehaired. Others, those with their backs to us, appear intact: we catch sight of ears and pigs' tails, but then take in the sight of bloody mouths. The very pinkness of them leaps out at us: rows of pink-fleshed dead pigs.

But smack in the middle of the photo of the meat locker is a nude white woman. She too hangs upside down. Her pinkness, too, leaps out at us. Her legs and armpits, like the pigs' bodies, are dehaired. Her ankles are bound together to attach them to the ceiling.

We know she is alive because this is a performance piece called *Average White Girl.* The circus/cabaret performer, Kirsty Little, said she was evoking the search for identity from a female point of view. Where did she search for a white girl's identity? In a meat locker, among dead pigs.

CATHY GOEGGEL

BRUCE BUCHANAN

Average White Girl meets Pork, the other white meat.

Why are the pigs depicted in advertisements pink? These advertisements are not only speaking about the "pink" of femaleness, they are speaking about whiteness, too.

In fact, pigs are many different colors: There are black and white pigs, chocolate pigs, nutmeg pigs. But with pink pigs, the inside and the outside are the same—pink outside, pink inside (though the pink is called "white").

DOUGLAS BUCHANAN

BENJAMIN BUCHANAN

Although a few leering customers might tell Lorene Cary—when she was the first African American waitress at a restaurant—that they preferred "dark meat," to sexualize pigs, pink pigs are used to recall white female flesh. (*Young* white flesh since the anthropornographed pigs have no explicit pubic hair.) Whiteness becomes the anthropocentric anchor, that which hooks it to the human side of the equation. A "colored" pig would tip the associations too far onto the Not-A side.

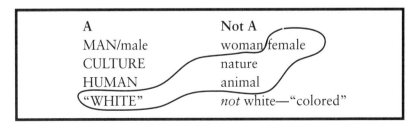

The pinkness of nonhumans in anthropornography highlights whiteness as a racial identity.

A friend told me a story about the time her brother brought a white girlfriend home to share the Thanksgiving meal with his African American family. As their nervous father carved the turkey's corpse, he turned to his son and asked, "Do you want white meat or colored?" Like the waitress-turned-writer Lorene Cary, they too were "back to black and white in America."

In chapter 11, "Anthropornography," I described A REAL CHEAP DISH and its pink stripper cow posed above those words. Underneath, half the size of the looming words, and just one-third the size of the pink sex object towering above, rising from the lower part of the page is a blue bull. Looking in a knowing way from underneath his Jack Nicholson glasses, he flexes his large muscle, and in doing so, calls attention to his strength. His muscular chest, with just a little hair, is clothed in an athletic T-shirt that proclaims BEEF-CAKE on its front.

He is power and strength, self-assurance. He is in command.

He might be a "dish"—that word is the only one that is near *his* image, but not cheap. No way. A small headline near him tells us, "With a little preparation, lesser cuts of meat can become great substitutes."

With a ring through his nose, he is the assurance that *we, (this kind of meat)* are *good* substitutes.

Did I say she is pink, he is blue?

Natalie Angier remarks, "Men grow up with the conviction that they are always stronger than somebody." (She observes this in a chapter on exercise and muscle entitled "Cheap Meat"). The something they are stronger than is *woman.*

She is *a* cheap dish; he's just working on his "cheap" meat—his muscle.

Did the *Seattle Post-Intelligencer* show men's strength juxtaposed with women's strength? Of course not. It's men's strength—beefcake or not—juxtaposed with woman as sex object.

Men *act*; women *appear.*

Men are strong; women are strong temptations, especially if cheap.

This is the difference between anthropornography and "beefcake." The bull in his Jack Nicholson glasses is in possession of himself. "A" possesses "A." There is no thrusting toward another. No signs of subordination. Men may be "beef" or "beefy" but woman/animal is meat/whore. Sexuality is not something she possesses, but is something that allows her to be possessed by another.

With anthropornography, man is in possession of another being; "A" possesses "Not-A." Someone has become something.

Herbert Muschamp, the architecture critic of the *New York Times,* devoted a celebratory article in the magazine section to a discussion of beefcake: "Bruce Weber's the Name, Beefcake's the Game." Bruce Weber's homoerotic photographs of "dressed-down male models" have encouraged men to turn to personal trainers and plastic surgeons for help in attaining "an implausibly trim physique." His photographs, declares Muschamp, do to men what has usually been done to women, with Weber the active subject, his photographed-male models the passive object.

Muschamp muses that Weber's photographs "subvert the hierarchy that values men for their achievements, women for their looks." Yet, Muschamp must ask: "At the same time, these images affirm the right of some people to turn other people into objects. Do we like objectification? Is it so different from necrophilia?" Making a subject into an object seems like a fetish for dead bodies.

But beefcake doesn't really make men objects in a way similar to women. Consider the British Boddingtons's beer advertisements that feature "Graham Heffer"—a male cow.

In the text that accompanies the advertisement that poses Graham as a cover story, Graham tells about his life since he became a "superstar" as an actor for Boddingtons. Puns abound, about "milking" the offers and "everybody

wants a piece of me." He concludes by saying he has joined a gym, and goes there every day since he has to stay in shape and he needs some "beefing-up."

Although on the one hand we have in Graham Heffer a sort of gender-bending performance piece, after all he is an anomaly—a *male* cow—the ads actually hold to several aspects of "beefcake." Anthony Cortese, who has analyzed advertisements, reports that "The ideal man in ads is young, handsome, clean cut, perfect, and sexually alluring. Today's man has pumped his pecs and shoulders and exhibits well-defined abs. . . . Shirtlessness is part of a trend that corresponds to the rise of the beefy male model."

Even Graham Heffer wants to triumph over femaleness—his own.

One final difference between "beefcake" and anthropornography is that men's "beefiness" in advertisements, even gender-bending Graham Heffer's, *usually sells something other than meat.*

In the Camel ad, men are supposedly being viewed as meat by cannibalistic women.

But what do we really have? White men in a hot tub with white women spa attendants.

This is beefcake: Muscularity. Ath-

letic. Wholeness. Self-possession. Muscle. Integrity has not been compromised. Sexual agency is there, and it is *his.*

"Beefcake" might suggest the illusion that women are equal to men in terms of entitlement over another's body. But beefcake is actually a confirmation of men's power. It is man-to-man language, too. Men's meat nature, "man stew," is enhancing. They are not fragmented by slaughtering or the cues of violability. They are not there to sell fragmented pieces of slaughtered nonhumans.

Here, too, we are back to black and white in America. The cannibal theme, when used in advertisements in the 1930s, featured depictions of Africans or African Americans preparing to eat whites. To place African Americans around an ad announcing "man stew" would now be seen as a recycling of racist attitudes. Cannibals were "savages" of the worst kind. Historically, the charge of cannibalism was used to legitimate colonial incursions that were going to save "savages" from their immoral behavior. And it became another way to confirm that African Americans were nearer to the gorillas than the (white) human. Rather than representing beast-like passions, white women provide a sign of domesticity to the cannibal theme.

The composition of the ad confirms that it is directed most importantly to men: they are the center of attention. One aspect of the message is *It's important to take care of men.*

We see again and again that beefcake is actually a confirmation of men's power, men's muscle. It has little to do with being a piece of meat.

In a discussion of the increasing nudity of women in mainstream films, the *New York Times* had to address the question of men's nudity. The terminology was revealing: women are *naked, nude, bare;* men are *uncovered.* When a man is shown nude, Suzanna Andrews reported, "the reaction is that he is extremely vulnerable." They may feel "anxious," "inadequate." Women's bodies become public; but men's bodies are to remain their private property. Even the slang definition of beefcake confirms this: The men aren't nude but "partially clad muscular men."

Lenore Rosenman, a psychologist, perceives that this is still "a society that protects men. . . . One way we do it is by not exposing them." She continues, "There is something of a power trip in stripping women and keeping men covered and safe."

The men are in a hot tub; yet, we, like them, are protected from their nudity.

"Beefcake" contains power. Perhaps one final reason that beefcake muscles itself above cheap cuts and pieces of meat is because normal, healthy adult males are rarely eaten in our culture. Meat eaters consume females, castrated males, and babies.

This "crate" keeps mother pigs from rolling over on their babies. If rolling over on their babies was a major problem, one wonders how it is that pigs did not become extinct before the twentieth century and this crate's invention. In fact, if they can, pigs build "nests" of grass, leaves, and straw.

JIM MASON

Farrowing crates are not nests, but a prison cell, limiting the sow's ability to nurture her young, and her ability to walk, or even turn around.

How is the sow's reproductive slavery appropriated within the world of sexual dominance? As though it were a plaything for a sadomasochist encounter.

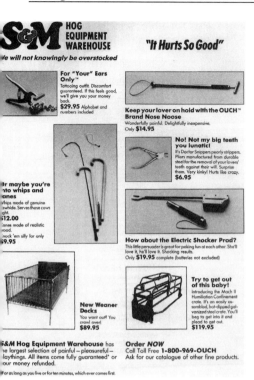

This *Playboar* "S & M" page takes all the tools used to control pigs and reinterprets them. "You'll beg to get into it and plead to get out" they playfully declare about *their* farrowing crate, implying that the pigs really like it and want more. This is a form of denial: *We aren't harming anyone!* Of course, the idea that farmed animals desire what happens to them is very comforting. This approach has worked for explaining the sexual exploitation of women. Why not blame the victims of our meat eating, too?

The existence of harm vanishes because it is fused to what men see: women (or pigs) "wanting" it.

It is hard for men to perceive the harm in sexual force and degradation because it has been made fun. The pig in a farrowing crate is being harmed. Her movements restricted, her access to her own babies controlled, her mothering under the tyranny of a controlling someone—a subject.

S & M, the "advertisement" informs us, is akin to the way humans treat farmed animals.

Playboar's choice of sado-masochism as the framework acknowledges that these implements are aspects of a dominating relationship to pigs. It is just *sexual* domination and that is fun. Human domination, which might hurt someone, fades as an issue.

On the following page is one final image of men as meat. Again, they retain power and wholeness. And as football players they reiterate the idea that the stronger women get (gaining some muscle?), the more men love football.

These football players are armored against their own nudity. Again, when men are "beefcake," no butchered flesh is visible. Like men's nudity, actual reminders of slaughtering must not occur. We might rephrase the psychologist's insight to say, "There is something of a power trip in showing women as meat but keeping men as beefcake."

Brandon Juhl, who noticed this ad and sent it to me, suggests that it indicates a tension in our view of football players. "Our macho, male-centered culture loves sports and sports figures, especially football, and yet it seems this ad signals that we also look down on them as being more brawn than brain, more like animals or cuts of meat who perform for our amusement and entertainment, modern-day gladiators."

The ad calls attention to men's bulk: how much each of them weighs—and not a one under 200 pounds. (The average female model weighs 23 percent less than the average woman.) If this ad were actually selling "meat" those numbers would represent their price per pound.

Notice one thing: Which so-called meat is the least expensive? Subconsciously, we are brought back to black and white in America. Or maybe we never left.

14

Hoofing It

ACTOR AND MODEL KELLY LYNCH reports that, "I think it takes someone really well-grounded to model and not feel like last week's barbecue. You're meat. People look at your legs and inspect your teeth. It's like the 4-H shows and you're one of the cows."

With 4-H shows and modeling, the meat is still *on the hoof*, that is, *not yet butchered, alive.*

Hockey "legend" Bobby Hull says of beef on the hoof: "If you can pick women, you can pick cattle. You look for good angularity, nice legs, and capacity." The television ad for a Red Lobster meal of dead crab legs, emphasizes the word *legs* while showing a shot of women running on the beach.

BAR-B-Q PORK RIBS
A hearty portion of our famous Rack-Attack ribs, served with a side of baked beans. 14.45

STEAK & SHRIMP
A tender steak flame broiled, with deep fried gulf shrimp. 12.65

Milan Kundera described the pig Mefisto in *The Unbearable Lightness of Being*: "he paraded around on his hoofs like a heavy-thighed woman in high heels."

At a roast honoring "famously sexy" food critic Gael Greene, gossip columnist Liz Smith described the problem with meat on the hoof, "It's just

so difficult to tie her two legs together for the roasting pan."

Of course, with captive turkeys, tying their legs together is much easier. To begin with, they are dead.

Beef on the hoof present a singular problem in today's world of mass meat production. Imagine cattle crowded together, bumping into each other in feed lots, standing amid their own pools of manure. This manure, this *fecal material,* may contain the *E. coli 0157:H7* bacteria, which can survive for ninety days in manure. Manure, sticky and wet, may adhere to the skin of cattle. Then they are slaughtered, with dried manure on their legs, on their tail, on their skin.

When their skin is removed, chunks of manure may fall off, or the skin may brush against another dead animal. The bacteria on one dead cow are transferred to another dead cow. Each dead cow may also contain the pathogens within them, in their stomach and intestine. Sometimes when the internal organs are being ripped from the body cavity, at the rate of one evisceration a minute, the stomach or intestines break. These pathogens can then splatter upon five other dead cows being processed into hamburger.

The result, as Eric Schlosser's *Fast Food Nation* tells us, is "there is shit in the meat."

A solution to the problem of manure on the hair on the skin of cattle has been proposed. Just as with women: use depilatories to remove the hair from the cattle.

Depilatories for removing hair from cattle had been tried in the 1970s, but their use was stopped because the meat-packing employees were losing their hair, eyebrows, and body hair. But in the 1990s, a new depilatory was developed, like the "foul-smelling depilatories women put on their legs to remove unwanted hair." This cream would be foamed onto cattle. After the cat-

tle are stunned and bled, the cream is foamed on, left for two and a half minutes, and then blown off.

As noted, shaving heads in the military, like shaving pubic hair, eliminates a sign of individuality. What about shaved legs?

According to John Berger, women's skin is stripped of hair to appeal to the male viewer's "sexuality, not hers." He continues, "Hair is associated with sexual power, with passion. The woman's sexual passion needs to be min- imized so that the spectator may feel that he

FRANK C. DOUGHERTY

has a monopoly of such passion. Women are there to feed an appetite, not to have any of their own."

Apparently so, too, are deer—there to feed someone else's appetite.

ROY SIZEMORE

The feminized legs and hooves on the preceding page were featured in an ad to help hunters hear "game" (i.e., live animals) and improve their hunting success. (Other electronic gadgets available for today's hunter include: ground-mounted motion detectors, binoculars with lenses suspended in fluid, stabilizing the image, a satellite-guided positioning system that keeps the hunter from getting lost, and chemically heated camouflage with thermal boots.)

The idea of deers' legs as women's legs is fulfilled on a "buckpole"—where captured beings are strung up.

High heels themselves are part of the message of subordination.

Why do men go to *streetwalkers?*

It's the excitement, that I drive there and find a girl who's good-looking. It's exciting to stop and to hear her steps in high heels. When you've discovered her and—well, the most exciting thing is when you've parked the car and then, maybe in the rearview mirror, you see that she's coming over, you hear the steps—oh my God, that is so exciting that I get . . . I start to sweat just thinking about it.

If the heels he hears stepping toward him are more than 5.7 cm high, they are distributing the street-walker's weight unevenly, stressing the spine, causing back pain, throwing off her center of gravity, thereby making running difficult.

The message of heels becomes, "we will gladly hurt ourselves for you."

Heels, especially stiletto heels, function as phallic symbols as well. *Penthouse* took the masochistic meaning of heels one step further, depicting a woman getting sexual pleasure from penetrating her genitals with a high-heel shoe.

Not only ourselves . . . we will hurt helpless

others, too. At least that is the recent message of a new genre of pornography called "crush videos" or "animal snuff movies" that emerged in the 1990s. (Snuff movies appeared in the 1970s and claimed to be showing the actual murder and disemboweling of a woman.) In crush videos, women in stilettos are shown crushing small animals—frogs, guinea pigs, kittens, monkeys, rats, mice—and even large insects like crickets to death.

While, at times, animals may be squeezed to death between breasts, generally animal crush videos follow certain conventions.

First, the small animal, for instance, a guinea pig is taped to the floor—perhaps spread-eagled, with each tiny leg taped down.

The camera, pulling back from that scene takes in a woman's legs from the knees down wearing stilettos.

Her soft, low voice creates the tension between the cultural notion of femininity and the power and control she has at this moment: "You are my victim. Are you frightened, little man? You know that your destiny is under my heels."

The sharp heel shatters the bones of one leg and then of another. Then, a toe crushes the guinea pig's back. Shoulder bones are trampled upon and broken. After about thirty minutes, the final blow occurs—the heel drives through the head into the skull.

At this precise moment, if the film has had its intended effect, ejaculation occurs for the male viewer.

"Choose your weapon."
−Kenneth Cole

This is an action right out of battering, where the issue is control. A batterer executes an animal to prove who has the power. It is an action right out of sadism, where the issue is the enjoyment of cruelty. We can imagine Stephen King's sadists doing something like this; in fact, *The Green Mile* uses a similar snuffing out of an animal to alert filmgoers to the sadism of a male guard.

This is an everyday action in relationship to "vermin" for some people.

What is interesting in this development of crush videos is not that animals are being killed in an inhumane way. That is everyday business. The news is that pornographers are interested in this. So the question is, *What are the makers and the users of pornography getting out of this?*

Some people get off on violence against animals: cockfighting remains legal in some parts of the United States; bullfights continue to draw spectators. Years ago, in New York City, an animal rights activist and filmmaker showed weekly videos to raise consciousness about what was happening to animals.

At first, he showed films that could be considered gory. "Bleeding Jesus" films, a Catholic friend calls them. Feeling uncomfortable about the footage, the filmmaker decided to show less graphic films. After that, he noticed that an entire group of men who had been faithful attendees for the more graphic films no longer came. Perhaps they started watching television nature programs that depict bloody carnivorous attacks on herbivores. (Considering that less than six percent of "wildlife" die in that manner, carnivores are overrepresented in these programs.)

Does this male thematics of gore explain crush videos?

No.

It has been suggested that men who enjoy watching crush films have a fantasy of themselves being crushed to death by a cruel, domineering female. In this analysis, the videos represent powerlessness, and appeal to people, especially heterosexual men, who wish to experience sex in this way. The animal has been so emptied of meaning in and of himself, he can represent another's suffering.

But the viewer doesn't weep over the tortured animal. He ejaculates. That masturbatory action must be central to our understanding.

What is unique about these films is that women are being used. Their presence creates the sexual message. The way to inject the message of sexual dominance is to include a woman. The woman telegraphs that this is sex. The truncated woman with the smooth legs and stiletto heels—for pornography, this is sex.

What is turning the men on? It is the power that is *presumed and absent* not the power that is being expressed. "I am so powerful that I can make a woman kill an animal to gratify my sexual needs."

Both pornography and advertisements situate men over women to show the power men have over them. Whether it is the 1960s' advertisement for a shirt or a pornographic-bondage photo, with a man leaning over a woman, the body language and vertical positioning exist to say, "We, men, are dominant." This situating of man over woman becomes such a given that the man can actually be missing from the image, yet we know where he is both by the positioning of the camera, and through the positioning of the woman or other cues of subordination. We know a man's power is being expressed, even if he is literally absent from the shot and even if the woman is shown with dominion over an animal.

Look at the Louis Vuitton shoes and the high heels on a "roast." *No one* appears to have caused the implied lynching of a woman or the actual death of a nonhuman. But someone has motivated these images of dominance, and someone killed the nonhuman.

The presence of women in crush films is what makes it pornography and what differentiates them from a run-of-the-mill film about animal abuse.

The films exploit the emotional conflict many humans have about whether animals are *someones* or *somethings* since the films presume that there will be a response—horror, fascination, awe—to what is happening to the animal. But women's debased status is something else entirely. She is needed there because the male users of pornography need her there—there with her heels on.

The presence of women confirms a fact about pornography: *It is always about power, even if the theme is powerlessness.* The Great Chain of Being—men are over women *and* animals—is forged once again through these videos. What turns the men on is knowing that there is this power over the women: the power to masturbate to women killing nonhumans. Anyone who can buy it or rent it or see it on the Internet is participating in the power of it, too.

In crush videos, pornography exploits two basic stereotypes: that women are supposed to be scared of mice and other small animals and that women are the ones who are supposed to care about animals. Clearly women have been the majority in animal activism. Pornographers have fun with the idea that women destroy animals rather than protecting them. But, they can have the fun since they have the power.

Chick 'n' Grill, below, and Zinpro, on the following page, tell us that women's legs and chickens' legs resemble each other.

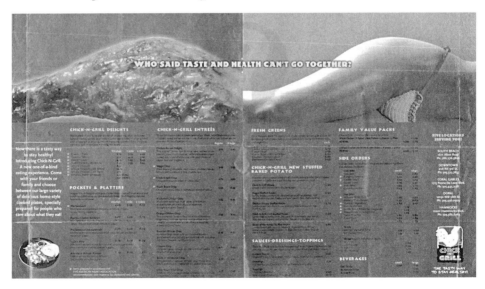

The idea that men's legs and women's legs might somehow be similar vanishes from consciousness.

The images in the Chick 'n' Grill advertisement announce THERE IS NO ONE THERE. Those legs without feet cannot run away. They can't hoof it; but then they aren't meant to—they are ornamentation, objects, waiting to be consumed. As the ad for Zinpro reminds us: *There'll be fewer condemned carcasses too!*

The tens of thousands of broiler chickens housed together either in completely or partially enclosed build-

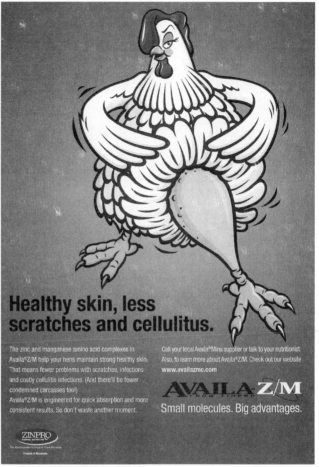

ings don't resemble the Zinpro sexy "chick." Bred to gain weight quickly, they would usually weigh a pound and a half at three months. Now they weigh nearly ten pounds.

They are so heavy that they cannot hold themselves up. Their lungs and hearts cannot support the fast growth. When they stand they tremble.

Because of the use of antibiotics in their feed, pigs, too, are brought to "slaughter weight" more rapidly. The rapid rate of growth causes skeletal deformities, arthritis, limb deformities, and joint problems. Pigs grow to be so big that their trotters cannot bear them. A drug used with pigs, Paylean, makes pigs more susceptible to becoming "downers." The pigs develop so much muscle that they become too stiff and are unable to move. There are now *double-muscled pigs* who have twice the muscle mass of a "normal" pig, and also suffer the same arthritis, joint, and limb problems.

**Downed cow left to suffer overnight in the
parking lot of a stockyard.**

Most downer cows are the byproduct of the dairy industry. Smaller, younger animals who have never given birth become downer cows when they are bred at a very young age. The trauma of giving birth when they are too young oftentimes causes partial or full paralysis in their back legs. Cows are often injured in transport because they are so tightly packed into the trucks, or through the loading and the unloading of the trucks.

The intense strain on older cows' bodies, producing ten times more milk than normal, pushes cows, often creating a metabolic problem. If they are sick, ill, exhausted, and unable to walk, they are supposed to be euthanized. Often they are not—it is still more profitable to slaughter them.

"Designer" slaughterhouses euphemistically called "Stairways to Heaven" are being built to trick the animals to walk to the proper location for them to be most efficiently killed. Downed animals, however, cannot walk to their death.

How does that off-the-hoof cow get to slaughter? The easiest way possible: pick her up in a front loader, drag her with chains, push her with a tractor or forklift.

She is not yet butchered, but neither is she hoofing it.

LESLIE DELLIOS, *OLIVIA ALWAYS KNEW!*

15

The Female of the Species

To CONTROL FERTILITY one must have absolute access to the female of the species.

For cows, sows, chickens, and female sheep, their reproductive and productive labor have merged. Their bodies must reproduce so that there will be "meat" for humans, so that there will be cow's milk for humans, so that there will be eggs for humans.

And so the "science" of animal agriculture has gone precisely where dominance goes—manipulating sexuality.

Consider the terms that exist in the English language for female animals whose reproductive labor serves human interests: *biddy, sow, bitch, hen, cow.* Not a positive word among them. These terms are as much critical of the *femaleness* of the animal as of the species they represent and are reproducing.

Jim Mason spent a day working in a turkey factory. "Bob," the boss in charge of artificial insemination told him, "We have to trick [the turkey] into laying all the time." An equipment catalog for artificial insemination provides instructions on this process of tricking the turkey:

The actual A.I. process itself should be at a rate that keeps the hens relaxed and calm, so that the hens will be more receptive to the semen and ensure a quality semination. With this relaxed pace, your birds won't struggle or fight you.

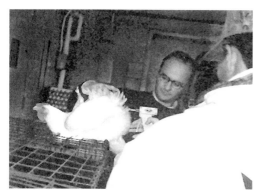

The process is a little more graphic than the catalog admits. Jim was put to work grabbing and "breaking" hens:

One "breaks" a hen by holding her breast down, legs down, tail up so that her cloaca or "vent" opens. This makes it easier for the inseminator to insert the tube and deliver a "shot" of semen.

That is why the animals exist—to be eaten. But the issue actually is *how?* By repeatedly forcibly impregnating female nonhumans. It is the speciesist version of keeping females barefoot and pregnant.

In order for the meat industry to profit from the female pig, she needs to produce three to four litters. But the sows are not physically able to last that long: between age, "reproductive failure," and lameness, sows are sent to slaughter earlier.

Sow: a fat, slovenly woman, a prostitute, a promiscuous young woman. A *sow* is diminished in the eyes of men both as a *pig* (species) and as a sex (female).

Meanwhile, researchers have been researching, as usual, on mice. In this case, they grafted a part of the uterus from one mouse into another. Now, one female animal can be doubly pregnant. Eventually, the researchers predict the procedure can be reproduced "in humans." By which, of course, they mean in *women.*

Here we go again. First they experiment on female nonhumans, trying this, trying that, and the next thing we know women also are becoming breeders helping scientists to manufacture human beings.

When reproductive freedom is restricted, women become men's "private factory farms" (in the words of Elaine Charkowski) mass producing an endless supply of consumer/worker/breeder/soldier units.

A multibillion dollar industry that makes money off of the bodies of others, that controls female sexuality, is obsessed with nipples and pregnancy, and uses vibrators. The line between the pornographer's world and the actuality of female animals' lives may be nonexistent. That is because looking is not just constituting "maleness" but "humanness," not just differentiating gender through species associations, but species through gender associations.

Think about the apes (including humans), sloths, sea cows, elephants, bats, and ungulates. We all have hair, three ear bones, and a four-chambered heart. Yet we are called *Mammalia*, though only one half of us have milk-producing breasts, and when those of us who do lactate, it is done for only a part of our lives.

All cattle can be called *cows*. Bulls can be called "cows." Steer—castrated bulls—can be called cows. Unless specifically identified as male, animals carry the attributes of the female of the species. The generic, unlike *mankind*, is female.

Male animals, when used for the reproductive interests of humans, become female, the taking of their sperm uses female metaphors. Recall the "milking" chair for "Tom" turkeys.

Species is gendered (animals are feminized) and gender, that is, woman, who carries gender identification, is animalized. Man transcends species; woman bears it. So do the other animals.

If one learns much about chickens' lives, it is not surprising that humans might assume they would promote the eating of beef. Three hundred million laying hens in the United States are crowded into wire cages. A hen needs 72 square inches simply to stand comfortably; but instead hens live, up to eight per cage, in a space that allows each one only about 48- to 54-square inches. They do not even have enough room to stretch out their wings.

A free bird would spend about sixty percent of her day foraging. Instead, they are deprived of nest boxes, dustbathing material, perches, and foraging opportunities.

"Forced molting," when hens are deprived of food for eight to twelve days, is done to "stimulate" them. After they have lost thirty to thirty-five percent of their body weight, they will, it is hoped, resume higher egg production.

From *chick* to *biddy*—one is measured by one's reproductive capabilities, which for an actual chicken will be only about two years, because by then she is *spent*, her body exhausted, no longer laying eggs.

"Spent" hens with their fragile bones and "poor" flesh, are not desired by the meat industry. Lacking "value," that is monetary value, these *old biddies* must be disposed of. They may therefore travel thousands of miles to slaughter or they may be packed alive into containers that are then bulldozed into the ground.

The *Dictionary of Euphemisms* says that *biddy* is *a woman with whom a man might copulate casually.* But the *Random House Historical Dictionary of American Slang* added this meaning as well: *a fussy or quarrelsome old woman.*

Chickens are much more intelligent than most people acknowledge. Mother hens will teach their chicks lessons about life and how to navigate in the world. Mother hens teach and chicks learn what to eat, how to drink, where to roost, and, if they can, how to avoid enemies.

Dick Clark's cartoon strip on February 25, 1996, offered this tidbit: *Where did Paul Simon get the idea to write "Mother and Child Reunion?"* From a chicken-and-egg dish at a Chinese Restaurant.

EAT
CHICKEN

Given her life as a living milk machine for humans, a cow might well say, "Eat chicken."

Milking is done *to* her rather than *by* her. Udders swollen (perhaps with mastitis, painful pockets of pus that form around the teats), they are seen as dull because they are confined to a stall, denied the opportunity to nurse and nurture their calves.

Eight months out of the year, forced to be both pregnant and lactating, a cow will be exhausted by five years, when she could live to beyond twenty. We have made her this way and then blame her for being this way. *Cow: fat, dull, plodding.*

The first definition for "cow" in the *Random House Historical Dictionary of American Slang*, is *a woman; [specifically] a prostitute.—usu[ually] used derisively.* Also, *one of a group of girls in a pimp's stable.*

ULTRASOUND HELPS REVEAL COW FALSIES is the headline in the business section of the *Des Moines Register*. The problem? "Bovine 'boob jobs'" are being used to cheat at cattle shows. Marilynn Marchione explains: "Dairy show judges wonder the same thing oglers do when they see a well-endowed female: Are those real?"

A 1993 *New Yorker* cartoon shows a man milking a cow. (A man! As though it's done by humans not machines.) The man says to the cow: "By the way, dollface, nice hooters."

A poem, circulating ad nauseum by E-mail, demonstrates how the male experience and the male viewpoint merge. It sets the scene: a dark night with the moon shining, and the speaker (clearly male) alone with a female, a female with blue eyes, soft hair, and he knowing "just what she wanted to do." He places his hands on her breast and she slowly spreads her legs apart:

> *And when I did it, I felt no shame.*
> *All at once, the white stuff came.*
> *At last it's finished, It's all over now,*
> *My first time ever,*
> *At milking a cow. . . .*

The poem suggests that the "got milk" campaign is actually a series of pornographic "cum" shots, recycled in a family entertainment vehicle.

Lindsay Spaar of West Virginia describes a television advertisement for Quality Checked Dairy:

A teenage boy gets online and goes in a chatroom. He types, "Hi, I'm Todd. What's your name?"

Pink letters pop up and we hear a sensual voice say, "Jennifer."

We see Todd's obvious delight: he's talking to a female.

Jennifer asks, "Do you like dairy products?" The boy replies, "Yes. I'm drinking milk now." She asks if the dairy products are Quality Checked brand, describes the logo, etc.

DANIELLE MARINO

He tells her his milk is Quality Checked, and she responds, "Ditto." The boy then asks "Jennifer" what she is wearing. She says, "Oh, a little black and white number." We then see "Jennifer"—a cow in a stall standing in front of a computer screen. The ad flashes back to the boy's room, where we hear the boy whooping in joy, presumably because he found such a sexy chat partner.

The teenage boy probably wasn't portrayed as a person of color because of the issue of lactose intolerance. Lactose intolerance, the absence of the lactase enzyme which enables the digestion of the milk sugar lactose, means that some people get abdominal pain, bloating, gas, and diarrhea from drinking milk.

The United States dietary guidelines call for two to three daily servings of dairy products though approximately ninety percent of Asian Americans, seventy percent of African Americans, seventy percent of Native Americans and fifty-three percent of Hispanics are lactose intolerant.

What will happen to "Jennifer" when she becomes a used-up, "old cow"? Let's ASK MARILYN.

Marilyn vos Savant, listed in *The Guinness Book of World Records* Hall of Fame for having the "Highest IQ," was asked if she would mind if a very smart calf (born as a result of newly acquired artificial-insemination skills) could be named for her? Marilyn's response: "Mind?! Why, I'm honored! But I sure hope 'Marilyn' is a dairy cow. I don't want to have to worry every time I look down at a plate of roast beef."

Where does the smartest woman in the world think dairy cows go when they are "spent"? To the Dairy Queen retirement home? The reason Mad Cow disease spread through cows was precisely because of their doubled use as reproducers and producer, as source of protein in life and in death.

Mad cow disease (bovine spongiform encephalopathy), like its human counterpart, takes several years to manifest itself. Cows are the only farmed animals kept alive long enough (until they stop "producing" milk) to manifest the disease. And then because they are also eaten, their diseased body becomes food for humans (and until recently) those parts that humans did not eat were fed back to cows.

Heavy women are known as *cows.*

An article from the *New York Times* featured a recipe they adapted from the *New England Journal of Medicine* for a low-fat, low-cholesterol ground meat. The recipe shows that the "meat" could be "beef," "veal," "pork," or "lamb." But though the text would allow it, did the artist choose to depict a male animal?

"I *used* to be an old, fat cow. See me in my 'before' shot?"

"But now I am thin and sexy . . . because I eat low-fat meat!"

The cannibalistic undertone of the picture, (*I've lost weight on this new low-fat diet of low-fat hamburgers*) reveals a canny understanding that cows had been made into cannibals.

What happens to the pretty young "thing" when she becomes the "old cow"? In *Feminine Forever* (1966), Dr. Robert Wilson tells us: menopause is a "living decay" that causes women to descend into a "vapid, cow-like state." But something could prevent old cows from becoming dull and unattractive: the urine of pregnant mares.

Just as Wilson never revealed that the funding for his book and for his energetic campaign on behalf of estrogen for menopausal women came from the main producer of estrogen, the fact that this estrogen was derived from keeping mares pregnant was not widely discussed.

HORACIO CARDO

Estrogen, this "wonder drug" (collected through harnesses with pouches that cup the genitals of pregnant mares so that they cannot lie down comfortably), was promised to take years off of women, keeping women young, sexually involved, attractive and as a consequence happy.

Menopause, a natural step in the aging process was pathologized. The young thing/old cow image could have functioned equally as an ad for Premarin.

In 1991, 45 million prescriptions for Premarin and 22 million for Prempro (Premarin with a progestin chaser) were filled in the US. For the tens of thousands of horses so enslaved throughout Canada and the United States, this meant yearly pregnancies, loss of their young foals (the necessary but unwanted consequence of pregnancy), who were removed to become horsemeat for Europeans, and often, standing in a small stall, encumbered by a urine-collection bag.

For the women who ingested mare's urine in the form of the top-selling brand-name pharmaceutical this meant elevated chances of breast cancer, heart attacks, stroke, and blood clots.

GIVE THE
GIFT OF
CHIKIN

CAROL J. ADAMS

In July, 2002, 16,000 participants in the Women's Health Initiative were abruptly told to stop taking hormone replacement therapy because it had been found that this therapy raises the risk of strokes by 41 percent, the risk of heart attacks by 29 percent, and breast cancer by 26 percent.

Soy products may provide natural isoflavones that could protect bones and phytoestrogens that reduce menopausal symptoms.

What prevents us from imagining that cows actually wouldn't wish their fate on anyone else? Their poor spelling. Their complete devaluation is telegraphed in their misspellings, because it reaffirms human superiority. The implication is that even if cows *could* spell they would never be able to spell as well as humans.

Why does "meat of wheat," a vegetarian product, show zebras, elephants, and giraffes escaping from the burger bun? Why aren't cows, chickens, turkeys, pigs, and lambs depicted? Because the farmed animals have so little status as individuals that few can recognize the harm to them in eating them.

Pigs, chickens, turkeys, cows, and lambs are so thoroughly *somethings* they can't represent their own need to be *someones*. A substitute had to be inserted to arouse sympathy. Similarly, when

ANIMAL FREE
MEAT of WHEAT

a man poses like the woman in the Versace ad in chapter 10, we are confronted with the oddness of a high-status individual posed as a sex object. Like a giraffe instead of a cow coming from a burger, a man in the place of a woman exposes how *someone* has become *something*.

The need to substitute giraffes and zebras for cows and chickens occurs because of circular reasoning: being devalued by the culture (e.g., "They're *only* chickens!") is taken as proof that they actually lack of value. What has been done to them is assumed to be the *cause* of the harm. As a result of such reasoning, harm to a now-degraded individual does not require our attention.

This is what happens with women who have been used sexually. Consider Linda Marchiano's experience as "Linda Lovelace," the coerced star of *Deep Throat*. She reports that she was forced—under threat of death by her real-life batterer—to allow a dog to mount her in the production of a pornographic movie. This was, she said, "the worst moment of my life." "From then on if I didn't do something he wanted, he'd bring me a pet, a dog."

Speaking of Linda Marchiano, Catharine MacKinnon points out that,

It is apparently difficult to carry on about the ultimate inviolability of the person in the face of a person who has been so ultimately violated. . . . If it happened and it hurt her, she deserved it. If she didn't deserve it, either it didn't happen or it didn't hurt her. If she says it hurt her, she's oversensitive or unliberated.

ove Ewe Close-Up

© Copyright Mutton Bone, Inc. All Rights Reserved.

Only $24.95 (plus shipping and handling)

Contempt is reserved—whether for the pig, the cow, the chicken, or for women—for the one done to, rather than the doer.

And so an advertisement brings us here—sexually receptive females.

The Love Ewe, according to its originators, was created as a joke, a gag gift, supposedly recognizing how shepherds, farmers and fraternity pledges "sought the comforts of a convenient sheep when a woman was unavailable."

Bestiality involving women occupies an entire genre in pornography. Bears, snakes, dogs, and insects—to name just a few species of animals—have been photographed or videotaped in a variety of sexual positions with women.

Sex "clubs" around the globe offer live scenes of sex between women and animals. Some towns along the US–Mexican border feature shows "starring" women and donkeys. Women of color are often depicted with animals as a way of enforcing the racist notion that women of color are insatiable. The idea of an African American woman having sex with animals, and all of its symbolism, isn't simply a historical artifact of slavery.

All the major pornography magazines at times insert a bestiality thematic. *Hustler* for instance, provided a ten page photo-essay in which a bear is shown at first licking a woman's stomach; by the end, he is licking her genitals.

A magazine like *Playboy* can't "show" bestiality or else it will lose its status as a mainstream media, so it maintains the theme of bestiality in an ongoing series of cartoons in which women are willing sexual partners of dogs, bears, and so forth.

Through pornography, dogs, snakes, and other animals, help a man picture himself in the scene. What the pornography consumer claims to be fantasy, we must regard as documentation of harm, especially for all pornography made before digital technology: a real woman must have a real snake inside her for a photograph of a snake inside her to exist, real cockroaches must enter real vaginas in order for a photograph of cockroaches in a vagina to exist, a real woman must give oral sex to a real bear in order for a photograph of a woman giving oral sex to a bear to exist.

There may be a stand-in for him, but this only increases the sense of omnipotence for the man watching. It feeds the sense of him that merges his omnipotence and his use of women as objects. This is why batterers, rapists, and other political terrorists force women under their control to have sex with animals.

Battered-women's shelters around the country receive reports from women who were forced to have sex with animals. Forced sex with trained dogs was a form of torturing Jewish women in Nazi Germany. It was recently used against female political prisoners in Chile.

Transgression of a taboo is itself a sexy act. Murder, cannibalism, incest, bestiality all are tabooed acts.

When advertisers portray the living animal, they draw on the pornographic positioning of women as

whores. But with the live animal as the sex object, bestiality—that tabooed act—is a referent point as well. Aren't these pornographed nonhumans inviting a sexual contact with a human penis?

When advertisers sell the body parts of butchered animals, we encounter the sexualizing of women's dismemberment. Cannibalism—*that* tabooed act—is a referent point.

Unlike ads for inanimate objects in which sexualization promises women, these meat ads promise woman plus something more, not just the unremembered, unacknowledged violation of a being, but violation of a taboo.

Violation of rules is sexy. Men are turned on by the taboo. Dominance reproduces itself in this way, too.

16

Male Chauvinist Pig?

ONE OF THE FIRST feminist demonstrations I took part in was to protest an all-male Boar's Head Dinner.

Two other feminists and I wrote a leaflet, mimeographed it, and stood in front of the doors to the main dining hall for undergraduates at the University of Rochester. As surprised male undergraduates, professors and administrators entered those doors, we handed them our leaflet.

The Boar's Head Dinner, ostensibly a celebration of the winter solstice, was not, in our view, an innocent enjoyment of male camaraderie. With a ritual carrying in of the head of a dead boar, it symbolically represented to us male dominance. It was male bonding over a sacrificial pig, common at pig roasts, taken to a new level.

Did I say *pig*? A boar is not just a pig, but an uncastrated one. Because their species is so thoroughly equated with femaleness, it requires the uncastrated male to be lifted up (on a platter) to elevate maleness, to celebrate the power of the inseminator in ritual or in images.

The *Playboar*.

This explicit maleness is required to distinguish the boar like the bull, from pigs, from cows. Also, the boar hunt provides a context of male bonding, in which the wild male is brought under cultural dominance, like the hanging of deer antler's in a home.

But something is happening even to boars in today's agricultural system.

THE BOAR'S HEAD DINNER
IS AN OBSTACLE TO
TO HUMAN LIBERATION

We are not condemning the Boar's Head Dinner
as an all-male gathering. It is important for
all of us to have contact and meaningful relationships with members of our own sex. What
we <u>are</u> objecting to is the use of women in
this event.

                        The primary role that women have
                        in this dinner is that of barmaid.
                        We find this role degrading because
                        it reinforces a typical stereotype.

We feel this dinner is part of the whole
socialization process which pressures men
and women into fulfilling <u>specific</u> <u>roles</u>.
Preconceived ways of acting limit the opportunity of each person to actualize her
or his potential as an individual.

                        In a time when women are struggling
                        for recognition as intelligent people
                        and not just as bodies or servants,
                        the Boar's Head Dinner is a real
                        obstacle to human liberation.

            Do you know that the budget for
            costumes alone for this dinner
            is $800 !

                  Enjoy your pig.

A boar at Cornell's breeding facility was named Arnold Schwarzenagger. With a "rape rack" to hold the sow in place, he would mount her and ejaculate. But he would almost pass out from the stress of it. He was so muscular he was close to being at the edge of not being functional.

The meal proclaims humans triumphant in their domination over the other animals. The part that telegraphs "I am someone"—the head, the face—is on display to confirm, *even you, you with a face, you, male animal, you are not someone when I say so. Your function is for me.*

In the Boar's Head Dinner, human maleness was affirmed through the procession of the boar's head (dead meat) and through the presence of barmaids (live flesh). Men over women and nonhumans.

Enjoy your pig we said. We knew what everyone would think—*male chauvinist pig.* We didn't have to say anything more.

Gloria Steinem explains that the hybrid coining of the term "male chauvinist pig" was an attempt to combine feminism with leftist rhetoric. The irony of drawing on the sexist left for a phrase identifying sexism is not lost on feminists. The term carried another ironic twist as well since the use of the term "pig" by the left to denounce illegitimate authority libeled pigs, who show no such misuse of authority (George Orwell notwithstanding).

Pigs are amiable, sensitive, and affectionate. As Joan Dunayer points out, "Boars rarely show aggression, even toward other boars, and are especially gentle with the young. A boar mates with a sow only if she is sexually receptive, after much mutual nuzzling, rubbing, and affable grunting."

Invoking pigs naturalized male dominance, as though men were behaving like nonhuman animals, as though the other animals behaved in that fashion.

Problematic, too, was that it dehumanized men, just as men had dehumanized women. By implying that

CAROL J. ADAMS INTERPRETING IMAGE AT HER SLIDE SHOW.
PHOTO BY JUAN GARCIA

"by being sexist you are no better than a pig," it relied on ideas of human separation from and superiority over the other animals.

Male chauvinist pig. As though one part of human male dominance isn't specifically its differentiation from the other animals, its refusal to see connections, its need to heighten differences, not just between women and men but between humans (read *men*) and animals (read *female*).

Male chauvinist pig. It failed to name male behavior for what it is, a unique expression of human male privilege constructed through cultural mediation. The fact is "pig" didn't stick to men in any helpful way because it was already stuck to women.

In the hierarchy of our culture, what intervenes between "man" and "pig" (and all other species) is "woman." Man the apex, woman the in-between, pig and other animals, the dehumanized. It was laughable to think of comparing men to pigs. Look up *boar* in slang dictionaries and there is no slang, because it is male. Women are both pigs (species) and sows (gender).

White men's *humanness* was so clearly delineated by evolutionary ladders and Great Chains of Beings and vertical-organization charts that it was not endangered by association with animals. *Bring out the boar's head. We can look it in the face. That is not our face, but that of the truly conquered.*

The dominance men express is not a dominance in which men are behaving like nonhuman animals; it is a dominance in which men are behaving as people with privilege, a privilege bestowed on them because of the inequality of gender and species.

The distance between "man" and "pig" was so great that the term *male chauvinist pig* became a way to belittle feminist analysis. Without ever saying, "Of course, we're not pigs; *women* are pigs," men and the media could have a great deal of fun with the idea. "Oh, I'm just a male chauvinist pig." (As though that took care of it.) Ties and pins announcing I AM A MALE CHAUVINIST PIG appeared.

One didn't have to seriously engage with the issue; instead it could be engulfed within male dominance. Trivialized. Just like the *Time* cover, "Are men really that bad?" The white-collar worker fixing his tie, so clearly not a "beast," not a "brute," heavens not a "pig," since the white-collar worker is not associated with any species identity except human —and human male (recall the Toshiba ad, pp. 48 and 58).

The message of the *Time* cover from the mid-1990s: *Of course we are not that bad, at least we don't think so. And anyway, we are so much more powerful to name what we are doing, we are so much more powerful because we have the power of mockery.*

The playful absorption of male chauvinist pig by the dominant culture revealed back then that men, white men especially, cannot be easily dehumanized. This confirmed that gender and species identification are not happening independently one from the other, they are happening interdependently.

Man is man because he isn't animal, woman isn't man because she is. And man isn't animal because he's not woman.

Enjoy your pig, we said, though we might have unthinkingly eaten pork chops that night. Like the feminists who protested the Miss America pageant back in 1968, we protested sexism, rather than human-male dominance. We did not see or understand the specific crime against the pig himself.

The way in which feminist analysis is made laughable didn't start with the reaction to male chauvinist pig. It started with that Miss America pageant of 1968. The invitation to protest clearly identified the coalition politics that has been fundamental to a feminist politic: welfare and social-work groups, peace groups, pro-abortion groups, black women's groups—all were invited to join in to protest "an image that oppresses us in every area in which it purports to represent us."

What Robin Morgan and the several busloads of women did the day that they protested the Miss America pageant was revolutionary: coming together as women to protest the treatment of women. Into their Freedom Trash Can went hair rollers, copies of *Playboy*, high heels, stenographers' pads, and of course, brassieres. But they did so connecting their protest to militarism, racism, and capitalism. Susan Douglas says what feminists did on that day was to link the "cultural to the political."

In *Where the Girls Are*, Douglas captures best how the media responded to this incredibly shocking political event. In the *New York Times*, for instance:

Throughout the article, the demonstrators were made to appear ridiculous, frivolous, and hypocritical. All the women's charges about sexism in the United States were placed in quotation marks, suggesting that these were merely the deluded hallucinations of a few ugly, angry women rather than a fact of life. The demonstrators' rhetoric was cast as highly inflated and thus absurd, and their complaints about female oppression seen as representing a wacky, self-seeking, publicity-hungry fringe of distinctly unrepresentative women. So the women who were protesting the public exhibition of women's bodies were themselves cast as nothing more than needy exhibitionists.

When, a year later, *Newsweek* referred to this demonstration as the one where women burned their brassieres, the media committed the body-chopping of a political idea.

Feminism became bra-burning. Nothing more, nothing less than yet another exhibitionist action by women. With the label *bra-burner*, as Douglas points out: "Women who threw their bras away may have said they were challenging sexism, but the media, with a wink, hinted that these women's motives were not at all political but personal: to be trendy and to attract men."

It's the wink that gives it all away. The power of the eye reestablished.

"Asking a man not to lust after a pretty young woman is like telling a carnivore not to like meat."

David Buss, an evolutionary psychologist, said this.

Natalie Angier describes the basic premises of what evolutionary psychologists like Buss believe. Men and women are the way they are because this is how we evolved; it was like this hundreds of thousands of years ago, they haven't changed, and they aren't going to.

Their tenets represent the overboundaried man's attitudes elevated to "science." Evolutionary psychologists believe: "Men are more promiscuous and less sexually reserved than women are. . . . Men are naturally attracted to youth and beauty [like Miss America's] . . . . Men are much more accepting of casual, even anonymous sex than women."

Right. Men want sex and steak because it's innate.

In 1999, Kitten Reynolds of Santa Cruz, California, continually harassed on the street by construction workers, finally had had enough. She made a costume that included smoked pork chops covering her breasts, and holding signs protesting sexual harassment walked outside Barry Swenson Builders, the employer of the construction workers. The Associated Press carried the story, which they called WOMAN'S DEMAND: I'M NOT MEAT!

Privilege is a difficult thing to perceive, like the vegetarian who likes a little meat on his women.

Advertisers, and not only meat advertisers, reassure human male self-identity, attitudes, and fantasies by objectifying them and re-presenting them back. They mystify the nature of personal identity, making it seem more fixed, less flexible than it actually is.

The privilege disappears and what the privilege allows access to—fun with the bodies of others—is seen only as a personal choice.

What is of concern is the social construction of men's privilege. The humanness and the maleness are locked together. That is what the advertisements reiterate.

Granting women equality with men is dangerous to the conception of "human," which relies on exclusion and to a sexuality that relies on dominance. What happens to the privilege that arises only through ignoring that humans *are* animals?

Can dominance relinquish its "fun" and discover the pleasure that comes from equality?

Not easily, as the advertisements by People for the Ethical Treatment of Animals show. Like other advertisers, PETA officials assume that they are speaking to "male chauvinist pigs" who use pornography and a media that wants "in" but can't quite do it themselves.

PETA draws on all the pornographic conventions that advertisers draw upon. They exploit the association of women and death. (*I'd rather be dead than wear fur.*) They project adult-male sexuality onto younger women (the Lolita model). They place women in cages, encouraging the human male to experience himself as superior.

In 1991, a judge ruled that by allowing the posting of pornography, Jacksonville Shipyards, Inc., created a hostile atmosphere for women that constituted sexual harassment. The judge called the pictures an unrelenting "visual assault on the sensibilities of female workers." Among the photos? One depicted a spatula pressing against a woman's genitalia; another a nude female torso with USDA Choice—the stamp of approval for meat—on it.

PETA's ads can be said to create hostile environments for women, reproducing the fragmented woman.

In their SOME PEOPLE NEED YOU INSIDE THEM campaign for human organ donors, they used "Playmate" Kimberly Hefner. Their goal was to limit testing nonhuman animals for cross-species organ donations. Concerning this campaign, PETA's Dan Mathews boasted in *Newsweek*, "Just because we are softhearted doesn't mean we can't be soft-core."

When Patti Davis posed with a dog (it was Hugh Hefner's dog), for a PETA campaign, PETA's press release boasted PATTI DAVIS TAKES IT ALL OFF FOR THE ANIMALS: DONATES HALF HER *PLAYBOY* FEE TO PETA.

Hugh Hefner is reported to have one of the largest collections of bestiality in the United States.

PETA used *Playboy* "playmates" Julie McCullough and Kari Kennell to serve vegetarian "Not Dogs" outside the halls of Congress to promote a healthy and humane diet. "*Playboy* is helping us put the 'T & A' in PETA," Dan Mathews, PETA's director of campaigns proclaimed.

They have also offered autographed copies of *Playboy* from their Web site.

Playboy sells women's inequality; PETA sells *Playboy*. PETA is selling women's inequality.

PETA recycles the idea of the "naturalized" man in hopes that one aspect of his behavior can be overcome (exploiting animals). Ironically, they implicitly endorse the idea that men's sexuality is animal-like, needing release through masturbation, and thus perpetuate a misunderstanding both of nonhuman animals and of sexuality.

PETA thinks nonhumans' oppression can be unmoored from being a part of men's privilege over others. Instead, entitlement remains entitlement, and ejaculation to pornography remains ejaculation to pornography.

PETA and other animal rights activists who defend the use of pornography fail to understand how dangerous it is to think that species can split from gender, to think that the category of species is not gendered.

Not addressing human male privilege allows many men to maintain their privilege to make someones into somethings while outwardly appearing to be compassionate.

PETA puts its women members at risk of being sexually harassed when they present their animal rights message. Howard Stern is only the most obvious person who asked PETA's women volunteers to *strip for the animals.*

PETA reaches out to adolescents while working with pornographers who sexualize youth and imply the acceptability of pedophilia.

It is not that PETA hasn't developed a stance about sexual ethics—it is that PETA has, and its stance is the same as the dominant culture's.

When, upon learning that he had killed his father and taken his mother,

Jocasta, for his wife, why did Oedipus put his eyes out rather than castrate himself? Psychotherapist Ellyn Kaschak answers the question:

It is by virtue of their gaze that men sin against women, that they objectify them, make them prisoners of appearance, of age and color, of physical beauty, of their shape and size. Only through blindness can such sight cease to oppress.

PETA assures men: *You need not put your eyes out.*

PETA tells us they know what they are doing. I believe them. They are shoring up manhood because they understand that it is threatened by the removal of species as a category to dominate. Sexual dominance must be reassured and intensified. They use the *gender that has been burdened with species to try to eliminate the oppression of species that have been burdened with gender.*

If animals are burdened by gender, by gendered associations, by the oppression that is gender, then they can't be liberated through representations of gender oppression. It isn't helping animals, and it certainly isn't helping men—to continue to believe that privilege is something to hold onto, even to masturbate to.

DAVID OLIVIER

So is this what I think? Are men *really* that bad? Do I think that all that men want is sex and steak and not necessarily in that order?

No. But it seems as though advertisers believe it. And pornographers believe it too. And so do many commentators: Better to caricature the critic by accusing them of caricatures then to examine the pleasure that comes from privilege.

In 1999, John Leo did a round up of "More PC Follies" for his *U.S. News and World Report* column. It included this one:

Well done, Carol. *Carol Adams, author of* The Sexual Politics of Meat, *argues that a meat-eating, patriarchal system oppresses animals and women*

alike. She told a University of Michigan audience that men seek power and
money primarily for "great sex and great meat."

One can almost see Leo's wink to his readers.

The previous Friday, Leo's fact checker had reached me at my parents' home. She asked me, "Did you say, 'men want great sex and great steak and not necessarily in that order?'"

I replied, "I was quoting directly from a woman's magazine."

"Well, did you say it?" the fact checker asked.

"I said it but I didn't *say* it. It was a quote."

With a note of desperation, she asked if I agreed with the ideas I was quoting. I said no, in fact I was criticizing them.

Early the following week, my father with some humor, handed me Leo's column as I ate breakfast.

That was fast! It must have been at the printer's before they had even "fact checked."

I called *U.S News and World Report* to find out why they bothered fact checking if they are going to print erroneous information. I was bounced to the head of the fact checkers. He said he would look into it.

A few days later they called to confirm that I had indeed told the fact checker her information was wrong. I was referred to an editor. And an editor's assistant. I told them there were plenty of my own beliefs that John Leo disagrees with. I would prefer to be criticized for what I do believe.

It was August. People were on vacation. As I delved my way through the various strata of personnel at that magazine, I learned a few things. In fact, many people were *very* helpful.

I was told that this was not the first time a problem with facts had occurred with Leo's column. (Like other right-wing columnists, Leo is sent clippings from college newspapers, scoured for them by local conservatives.)

I was told that Leo himself was not available. He was on vacation in the Southwest. He could not even be reached by telephone because he was *birding*.

A man who enjoys slamming animal activists is unavailable because he is watching *birds*.

Then I was told no correction could be issued without talking to him, no corrections are issued since he is a columnist.

It is so much easier to mischaracterize. If we are puritans, against the "sins" of the flesh (sex and steak and not necessarily in that order) then the issue is *my* problem, *my* hang up, not a political problem. The notion that we are moralizing, controlling, creates the desire for taboo-breaking, and taboo-breaking is itself eroticized. Taboos aren't about politics.

Since it is assumed that the essence of (male) sexuality is that it must be released, attempts to "control" sexuality are seen as destructive. Meanwhile, challenges to meat eating are seen as infringements on someone's *pleasure*. A political analysis about species and gender inequality is reduced to being repressive and controlling—whether about food or "sex."

By keeping the issue at the level of "pleasure" and "taboos," critics—whether conservative commentators like Leo, pro-pornography defenders, and/or users of animal foods—continue to speak the language of advertisers. The language of appetites and clichés ("bra-burner," "male chauvinist pig," "vegan police") keeps us safely circulating within the world that advertisers create.

When inequality is structured into our lives, it disappears as a privilege and is experienced as "desire," as "appetite," as pleasure.

Pleasure is unmoored from the privilege that permits it.

And the loss of privilege is felt as a loss of identity since they have merged.

In a culture that assigns different status to men and women and to mind and body, it is difficult for those with privilege to comprehend the meaning of the violation of bodies. We will call it, after Catharine MacKinnnon, a neo-Cartesian mind game—named for the philosopher who believed non-human animals were "machines," so that their cries when being tortured were never interpreted as evidence that in fact they were truly being tortured. The idea that they were automatons carried more weight than the bodily sensations that demonstrated that they were not.

This mind game is a function of human male privilege that enables a standpoint that views everything as being made out of ideas, out of abstractions.

From this vantage, pornography is an idea, a speech, rather than an act, a documentation of torture. For instance, Linda Marchiano ("Linda Lovelace") testified that she was forced into making pornography. Pornography like *Deep Throat* is evidence of her harm. But it is seen as an idea and protected as speech, while her statements about her sexual slavery, *Ordeal,* are sued for libel.

Meanwhile, the image of screaming, suffering carrots, lettuce, and tomatoes is invoked to justify why it is OK to be meat eaters.

Carrots are harmed but women used in pornography aren't. And so everything remains an idea and whatever is an idea is protected as speech.

In fact, several areas of speech are not protected. As Maria Comninou points out:

Shouting "Fire!" with no reason in a crowded theater, giving an attack command to a specially trained guard dog, giving unlicensed medical advice, false commercial advertising, soliciting bribes, criminal conspiracies, threats, contracts that violate the law—none of these is currently protected as free speech, and nobody is complaining.

Laura Lederer clarifies why no one complains about these "infringements" on speech:

once as a society we agree that a certain category of speech is harmful, we are likely to give it a label other than speech: e.g., "stick 'em up" becomes robbery; shouting fire in a crowded theater becomes incitement to riot; speech violating a trademark is an intellectual property matter; and so on.

First Amendment rights to speech are not absolute, but to maintain the idea that they are, unprotected speech is renamed as something else.

This is exactly what has happened with antihunting activism. Walking in the woods and shouting to protect nonhumans from hunters which clearly *is* speech, is not viewed as speech, but has been named "hunter harassment."

Laws to prevent the speech of animal rights activists (most of them women) now exist in all fifty states.

Free-speech advocates must ignore the harm that is claimed about pornography (the harm in the making and in the using) to protect it as speech; what harm, though, is caused by animal rights activists? The harm to hunters who are deprived of their targets?

Anti-abortion protesters who block entrances to abortion clinics—their activities are protected as speech.

Animal rights activists who enter the woods and seek to protect nonhumans—their activities are outlawed as conduct.

The feminist challenge to pornography isn't about obscenity or morals, but about politics. So, too, is the challenge to using animals as food.

For men to resolve the oedipal complex created by a patriarchal culture they must relinquish grandiosity and engulfment. Each man needs to experience boundaries—to know where he ends and others begin. He must replace a fragmented vision with a holistic one, one in which, in Ellyn Kaschak's terms, he "can look at women as full persons rather than as fetishized parts." He must no longer be "driven by power needs, sexually or in other ways." He must be able to face his own existential separation. He must discover "that he is not a king, just a human being in a world of other humans and other living creatures, all of equal importance to him."

EVANDER LOMKE

CAROL J. ADAMS

The only way these statements are anti-pleasure is if you get your pleasure from inequality.

It is not a matter of putting out one's eyes. It requires seeing the same thing differently.

It requires seeing *someone*, not something.

THERE'S A WORLD OF SUFFERING IN EVERY BITE OF MEAT

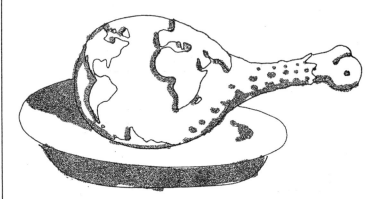

The misery in meat is food for thought. The preferred meal of affluent societies is a proven killer linked to cancer, heart disease and diabetes.

It kills people in other ways too. The grain which fattens animals for our dinner tables is oft times "appropriated" from the peoples of Third World countries; it enriches dictators while vast populations starve.

Meat production destroys the environment, squanders dwindling water reserves, pollutes our rivers and lakes with toxic animal wastes, and is causing the destruction of rain forests.

Greed for super-profits has relegated animals to the status of machine parts. Veal calves live out their entire lives in dark wooden crates, unable to even turn around.

Egg-laying hens are confined to an area smaller than this page. Factory-farmed animals are so stressed that only a constant diet of drugs keeps them alive until slaughter.

Beyond satisfying our addiction, meat has no demonstrable benefits. It creates unending suffering for people, destroys the environment and inflicts horrendous pain on more than six billion animals consumed in this country each year.

Only you can do something about the misery in meat. Cut it out or cut it down. You'll be taking a bite out of misery.

This ad was produced by the Coalition for Non-Violent Food, a project of Animal Rights Int'l., Henry Spira, coordinator. For more information on factory farming send SASE to: ARI, Box 214, Planetarium Sta., New York, NY 10024.

PETA

HERE'S THE BEEF!

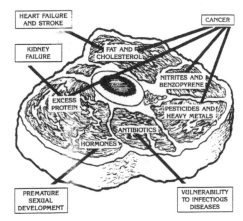

FARM

THE MEAT-EATER

MOO 2, ERIC REINDERS

SISTER

FEMINIST VEGETARIAN

ECSTATIC ~VEGETARIAN~ FARMER TAKES COW TO ~MARKET~ MOVIES

FEMINISM and MEAT EATING

A contradiction in terms!

Feminists for Animals Rights

Send your clippings, ads, photos, menus, matchbooks, magnets, and other images to Carol J. Adams c/o Continuum International 15 East 26th Street, New York, New York 10010

EPILOGUE

JUAN GARCIA

Acknowledgments

I AM GREATLY INDEBTED TO activists, scholars, readers, friends and family. To those who sent me illustrations—especially those who took the time to stop and take a photograph—thank you for such interesting mail! To activists who have worked to end violence against women and the other animals, thank you for your persistence. To scholars and writers who have taken the time to think and write about these issues, thank you for your insights and your dedication. Writing about violence is not an easy task at all; one wrings the tears out of one's pages at the end of each day. For my family and friends who have supported my passion, thank you for embracing my work and me. I appreciate the opportunity provided by *Animals' Agenda*, *Ms.*, and Feminists for Animal Rights to explore a few of these ideas in their publications.

I wish to acknowledge Harriet Schleifer for her pathbreaking review of Andrea Dworkin's *Pornography*, Linda Lovelace's *Ordeal*, and *Not a Love Story: A Film about Pornography* in 1982 in [*Animals'*] *Agenda*.

I am thankful for all of the staff of the Richardson Public Library, but especially Marilyn Comte and the Interlibrary Loan department, who have helped me research articles, advertisements, and obtain needed books.

My book is enriched by the work of the artists Sue Coe, Leslie Dellios, Nancy Hild, Penny Siopis, and Jo Spence. For their work resisting the dominant viewpoint, I am deeply grateful. Thank you to Terry Dennett of the Jo Spence Archives for supporting this project.

This book would not be possible without the readers of *The Sexual Politics of Meat* who sent me photographs, posters, T-shirts, greeting cards, matchbooks, cartoons, magnets, menus, newsclippings, and other ephemera they encountered in their daily lives. Susan kae Grant truly initiated this project by offering to make slides of the images that appeared in *The Sexual Politics of Meat* and *Neither Man nor Beast*, and then arranged for the first "slide show" at the National Conference of the Society for Photographic Education American in March, 1995.

In specific I wish to acknowledge the following people who have supported my work, by sending me images and/or through conversations: Sue Abromaitis, Muriel Adams, Carol Ames, Keith Akers, Lisa Alexander, Steve Baker, Patricia Barrera, Batya Bauman, Gene Bauston, Bonnie Berry, Rynn Berry, Nancy Bischof, Patti Breitman, Diana York Blaine, Dirk Boeckx, Benjamin Brenkert, Baird Callicott, Elaine Charkowski, Maynard Clark, Merritt Clifton, Glen Close, Nikki Craft, Lee Craig, Emily Culpepper, Karen Davis, David del Principe, Josephine Donovan, Tim Doucette, Howard Edelstein, Cynthia Eller, Stacy Erickson, Robert Faeder, Georg Feuerstein, Trisha Lamb Feuerstein, Mary Finelli, Lisa Finlay, Beth Fiteni, Marie Fortune, Kathy Frith, Mike Furlong, Anne Ganley, Greta Gaard, Lynn Gale, Andy Glick, Jennifer Goolsby, Jon Grindell, Suzi Parks Grissom, Megan Hagler, Amie Hamlin, Carole Hamlin, Daniel Hammer, Brian Hageman, Molly Hatcher, L. Herrick, Alex Hershaft, Maho Hisakawa, Mary Hunt, Dawn James, Pattrice Le-Muire Jones, Brandon Juhl, Tracy Kalkwarf, Susanne Kappeler, Robin Karell, Gus Kaufman, Scott Keating, Marti Kheel, Christina Kirkpatrick, Patrick Kwan, Tai Little, Jayne Loader, Sheri Lucas, Brian Luke, Cathleen McGuire, Jacinta Mack, Chaone Mallory, Danielle Marino, S. Leigh Matthews, David Meltzer, Manuela J. F. Menezes, Allison Miller, Liz Monnin, Doug Muller, Justin Natoli, Diane Neu, Ingrid Newkirk, Wayne Pacelle, Susan Peppers, Mary Principe, Liz Randol, Jinendra Ranka, Samantha Raue, Kevin Read, Marguerite Regan, Tom Regan, Estiva Reus, Pamela Rice, Xochi Rick, Michelle Rivera, Bina Robinson, Martin Rowe, Diana Russell, Janelle Ryznar, Mike Scar, Sarah Schmidt, Carolyn Schwartz, Kamber Sherrod, Kristine Simon, Sarah Jane Smiley, Lindsay Spaar, Dan Spencer, Mary Zeiss Stange, Eileen Stark, Lynn Starner, Kim Stallwood, Vicki Stevens, Kim Sturla, Deborah Tanzer, Angus Taylor, Cookie Teer, Emily Thomas, Michael Tillman, Nancy Tuana, Bernie

Unti, Jan Valois, Melinda Vadas, Rosemary Anne Waigh, Karen Warren, Mischa Warren, Zoe Weil, Christine L. Williams, Delora Wisemoon, Lora Woollven, Andrea Yandreski, lagusta yearwood, Gary Yourofsky, and Agnes Zawadzka. In addition, I benefited from the many readers of *Ms.* who contributed to their "No Comment" section over the years. I am also thankful for the staff of BWC who have made the images into slides, especially Cindy Newton, Monica Schwartz, and Lynn Starner.

Thank you to students and professors who have invited me to show the slide show on their campus and with whom I have had fascinating conversations. I have learned from discussions with students, faculty, and community members at Agnes Scott College, Augustana College, Bowling Green University, California State Polytechnic University at Pomona, Cal-Tech, Clark University, Concordia University, Canada, Cornell University, Deerfield Academy, Denison College, Gustavus Adolphus College, Hamline University, Kent State University, Lewis and Clark College of Law, Marist College, Mt. Holyoke, New College, University of South Florida, Northwestern University, Oberlin College, Ohio University, Ohio Wesleyan, Oregon State University, Pennsylvania State University, Portland State University, St. Cloud University, Scripps College, Seattle University, Sheffield University (England), Skidmore College, Smith College, State University of New York at Binghamton and at Fredonia, Southwestern University, Tufts University, University of Illinois, Champaign, University of Cincinnati, University of Florida, University of Maine at Orono, University of Michigan, University of North Texas, University of Oregon, University of Pittsburgh, University of Redlands, University of Rochester, University of Tennessee, University of Texas at Arlington, University of Texas at Austin, Virginia Tech, and Yale Law School. I have also learned from conversations with animal activists and vegetarians at the World Vegetarian Congress, 2000, the North American Vegetarian Summerfest, 2001 and 2002, the Animal Rights conferences, 2000 and 2001, the Michigan Federation of Humane Associations and Animal Advocates, 1997, and the student animal rights conference, Liberation Now, 2002 and 2003. Thanks especially to Amie Hamlin for coining the term *anthropornography.*

For help in transforming this book from a slide show to completed book, I am indebted to Helen Song, production manager at Continuum, Gabriella Page-Fort, and Coghill Composition Company. Pat Davis supported my vision, and John Stoltenberg, Robin Morgan, and Diana Russell provided direct inspiration for the work. Other antipornography activists and theorists inform these pages, especially Catharine MacKinnon, Andrea Dworkin, and Nikki Craft. I am grateful for the work of photographers Micha Gaus and Myron Brody, and thank them for the use of their photographs on the front and back cover of this book, respectively. Thank you to Patti Breitman and Werner Mark Linz for their simultaneous suggestion of the title. I benefited from the comments of the readers of this book in manuscript—Keith Akers, Patricia Barrera, Pat Davis, Pattrice le-muire jones, and Mary Hunt. My parents and my sisters have provided important support along the way.

Finally, thank you to my editor Evander Lomke, my partner Bruce Buchanan, and our children Doug and Ben Buchanan, not only for their role as photographers, but for sustaining the work and the writer.

Copyright
Acknowledgments

The author and publisher gratefully acknowledge the following:

Charlie, "Sausage made before your very eyes!" Copyright © Tribune Media Services, Inc. All Rights Reserved. Reprinted with permission.

"What pornography?" Source: *Women Against Pornography Newsreport*, x, no. 1 (summer 1993).

"More than Meat" postcard from TransSpecies Unlimited.

"Will work as food." Copyright © Mark Stivers. Reprinted with permission.

Giant hamburger. Melbourne, Australia, 1994. Copyright © Marie Fortune.

Photographs of butchered cow's heads, chicken slaughterhouse workers, chickens hanging upside down, veal calves and the graphic "Here's the beef." Copyright © Farm Animal Reform Movement (FARM). P. O. Box 30654. Bethesda, MD., 20824.

"Very vegetarian and *Hustler* cover," "Promote tolerance and Time cover," and "Same thing differently." Copyright © Juan Garcia.

Richard Nixon and Nikita Kruschev, by Elliott Erwitt, used by arrangement with Magnum Photos.

"Tasty Chick," Carl's Jr., near Sacramento, California, March 1997. Copyright © Marika Holmgren.

Nancy Hild, *Chicken, Bitch N' Bunny*, copyright © 1990. Used with permission of the artist.

Citations

p. 11. *"maison's d'abattage"* in Kathy Barry, *Female Sexual Slavery* (Englewood Cliffs, NJ: Prentice Hall, 1979), p. 3.

p. 12. Terrence Rafferty, "Solid Flesh: The Prince of Denmark, and the king of sleaze." *The New Yorker*, January 13, 1997, pp. 80–81.

p. 14. Liberty Police Department "Statement of Probable Cause," Case: 20021740. Offense: Animal Abuse. Date of Offense: 07-12-02, p. 1.

p. 15. F. K. Plous, Jr. "How to Kill a Chicken—and notes on the demise of the live poultry business." *Reader: Chicago's Free Weekly*. January 18, 1980 (9, no. 16: 1), p. 24.

p. 16. Peter Kramer, *Listening to Prozac* (New York: Viking, 1993), pp. ix–xi.

p. 18. Fred Weir, "Breasts for the West: Russian Stripper Market." *Guardian*, March 18, 1992, p. 14.

p. 19. Betty Debnam. "All about Sheep." *The Mini Page*. Universal Press Syndicate, 1990, page A.

p. 21. Sandra Lee Bartky, "Toward a Phenomenology of Feminist Consciousness," in *Feminism and Philosophy*, ed. By Mary Vetterling-Braggin, Frederick A. Elliston, and Jane English (Totowa, New Jersey: Littlefield, Adams and Co.), p. 26.

p. 22. "The Case of the False Mass Term," in my *Neither Man nor Beast* (New York: Continuum, 1994), pp. 27–30, explores this concept in greater detail.

p. 23. Tad Friend, "The Artistic Life: Kidnapped? A Painted Cow Goes Missing," *The New Yorker*, August 21 & 28, 2000, p. 62.

p. 23. *The Sexual Politics of Meat* (New York: Continuum, 1990), pp. 53–56, introduces my theory of the absent referent.

p. 27. "Elliot Erwitt: Nikita Krushchev and Richard Nixon's 'Kitchen Debate.'" *New York Times Magazine*, June 9, 1996. p. 123.

p. 27. Yelstin quoted in *Newsweek's* "Perspectives," April 8, 1996, p. 23.

p. 29. Marc Santora, "New York's War on smut won't end." *New York Times* article carried in the *Dallas Morning News*, August 1, 2002, p. 7A.

p. 29. Nancy E. Schaadt, "Pollo Fiesta: Great Place to Pick up Chicks," *Dallas Mornings News*, July 2, 199, p. 31.

p. 31. "The first rule . . ." in Rick and Gail Luttman, *Chickens in Your Backyard: A Beginner's Guide* (Rodale Press, 1978), p. 101.

p. 33. John Berger, *Ways of Seeing* (New York: Penguin Books, 1972), p. 47.

p. 33. Ellyn Kaschak, *Engendered Lives: A New Psychology of Women's Experiences* (New York: Basic Books, 1992), pp. 132–37.

p. 34. Mariah Burton Nelson, *The Stronger Women Get, the More Men Love Football: Sexism and the American Culture of Sports* (New York: Harcourt & Brace, 1994).

p. 34. Dotty Griffith, "Male Call: Bob's Outpost Replicates the Original's Masculine, Meaty Formula." *Dallas Morning News Guide*, May 31, 2002, p. 6.

p. 36. Roger Porter, "Prime Time." *Willamette Week: Portland News and Culture.* 23: no. 26. April 30, 1997. p. 41

p. 38. Elaine Tyler May, *Homeward Bound: American Families in the Cold War Era* (New York: Basic Books, 1988, 1999), pp. 10–11.

p. 39. William O'Barr, *Culture and the Ad: Exploring Otherness in the World of Advertising* (Boulder: Westview, 1994), p. 4.

p. 41. Andrea Dworkin, "Pornography Happens to Women," in *The Price We Pay: The Case against Racist Speech, Hate Propaganda, and Pornography* (New York: Hill and Wang, 1995), p. 187

p. 41. Bonnie Smith, *The Gender of History: Men, Women, and Historical Practice* (Cambridge, MA: Harvard University Press, 1998), p. 5. See also Genevieve Lloyd's *The Man of Reason: "Male" and "Female" in Western Philosophy* (Minneapolis: University of Minnesota Press, 1984), pp. 93–102.

p. 42. James is quoted in Una Stannard, *Mrs. Man* (San Francisco: GERMAINBOOKS, 1977), p. 2.

p. 43. Geneva Smitherman, *Black Talk : Words and Phrases from the Hood to the Amen Corner* (New York: Houghton Mifflin, 2000).

p. 43. Elizabeth Cady Stanton and the Revising Committee, *The Woman's Bible* (New York: European Publishing Company, 1898. Reprint, Seattle Coalition Task Force on Women and Religion, 1974).

p. 44. Keith Schneider, "Triple Murder Causes Alarm about Hate Group's Growth," *New York Times*, March 6, 1995, p. A10.

p. 45. Toni Morrison, *Playing in the Dark: Whiteness and the Literary Imagination* (New York: Random House, 1993), pp. 38, 57.

p. 46. On how racial myths keep sex tourists from admitting prostitutes are prostitutes for the money, I am indebted to the work of Julia O'Connell Davidson, *Prostitution, Power and Freedom* (Ann Arbor: University of Michigan Press, 1999), pp. 178–79.

p. 46. Irving Goffman, *Gender Advertisements* (New York: Harper and Row, 1979).

p. 47. Catharine MacKinnon, *Toward a Feminist Theory of the State* (Cambridge, MA: Harvard University Press, 1989), p. 122.

p. 47. Susanne Kappeler, *The Pornography of Representation* (Minneapolis: The University of Minnesota Press, 1986), p. 53.

p. 49. Katherine T. Frith, "Undressing the Ad: Reading Culture in Advertising." In *Undressing the Ad: Reading Culture in Advertising*, ed. Katherine T. Frith (New York: Peter Lang, 1997), pp. 1–14.

p. 50. Andrea Lewis, "Looking at the Total Picture: A Conversation with Health Activist Beverly Smith," in *The Black Women's Health Book: Speaking for Ourselves*, ed. Evelyn C. White (Seattle: The Seal Press, 1990), pp. 175–76.

p. 52. Carolyn Merchant, *The Death of Nature: Women, Ecology, and the Scientific Revolution* (San Francisco: Harper & Row, 1980), pp. 214, 193.

p. 52. Charlie LeDuff, "At a Slaughterhouse, Some Things Never Die: Who Kills, Who Cuts, Who Bosses Can Depend on Race," *New York Times*, June 16, 2000.

p. 53. Dick Gregory with Robert Lipsyte, *Nigger: An Autobiography* (New York: E. P. Dutton, 1976), p. 16.

p. 54. Quotes from white racist writings found in George M. Fredrickson, *The Black Image in the White Mind: The Debate on Afro-American Character and Destiny, 1817–1914* (New York: Harper & Row, 1971): "a fiend . . ." the words of Ben Tillman are on p. 276, "a knock is heard" the words of George T. Winston p. 278, and Dixon's words are on p. 281.

p. 55. Donald Bogle, *Toms, Coons, Mulattoes, Mammies, and Bucks: An Interpretive History of Blacks in American Films,* 4th ed. (New York and London: Continuum, 2001), pp. 13–14.

p. 55. See discussion of false charges of rape in Jacquelyn Dowd Hall, *Revolt against Chivalry: Jessie Daniel Ames and the Women's Campaign against Lynching* (New York: Columbia University Press, 1979).

p. 56. Susan Estrich, *Real Rape* (Cambridge: Harvard University Press, 1987), p. 1.

p. 56. Kate Clark, "The Linquistics of Blame: Representations of Women in the *Sun's* Reporting of Crimes of Sexual Violence," in *The Feminist Critique of Language* (London and New York: Routledge, 1998), pp. 183–197.

p. 57. Anita Hill quoted in Timothy M. Phelps and Helen Winternitz, *Capitol Games: The Inside Story of Clarence Thomas, Anita Hill, and a Supreme Court Nomination* (New York: Harper Perennial, 1993), p. 315.

p. 59. John Tierney, "Porn, the Low-Slung Engine of Progress," *New York Times*, January 9, 1994, Section 2, pp. 1, 18.

p. 61. Patricia Hill Collins, *Black Feminist Thought: Knowledge, Consciousness, and the Politics of Empowerment.* Tenth Anniversary Edition (New York and London: Routledge, 2000), pp. 134–43.

p. 61. T. Denean Sharpley-Whiting's *Black Venus* (Durham, NC: Duke University Press, 1999), provides this translation, p. 21.

p. 62. Rynn Berry, "IVU's 35th World Vegetarian Congress at Edinburgh," *VegNews*, September 2002, p. 12.

p. 62. Natalie Angier, *Woman: An Intimate Geography* (New York: Anchor Books, 1999), p. 54.

p. 64. Stephen Jay Gould, "The Hottentot Venus," *Natural History* (October 1982), p. 25.

p. 64. Londa Schiebinger, *Nature's Body: Gender in the Making of Modern Science* (Boston: Beacon Press, 1993), p. 166.

p. 65. Sander L. Gilman's *Difference and Pathology: Stereotypes of Sexuality, Race, and Madness* (Ithaca and London: Cornell University Press, 1985) discusses how Sarah Bartman had been reduced to her sexual parts and the linkage with the bustle, p. 91.

p. 67. Sharpley-Whiting, p. 31.

p. 68. "Raping a woman . . ." David Finkelhor and Kersti Yllo, *License to Rape: Sexual Abuse of Wives* (New York: Holt, Rinehart and Winston, 1985), p. 36.

p. 70. Cuvier quoted in Sharpley-Whiting, p. 28.

p. 75. Joby Warrick, "Modern Meat: A Brutal Harvest. 'They Die Piece by Piece.' In Overtaxed Plants, Humane Treatment of Cattle if Often a Battle Lost." *Washington Post*, April 11, 2001.

p. 75. "The enemy . . ." Larry Gallagher, "Meat Is Murder." *Details.* (March 1996). p. 152.

p. 77. Cecilie Høigård and Liv Finstad, *Backstreets: Prostitution, Money, and Love* (Pennsylvania: Pennsylvania State University Press, 1986, 1992), p. 64.

p. 79. Joan Acocella, "My Ex-husband and the Fish Dinner." *The New Yorker*, December 11, 1995, p. 120.

p. 80. Marilyn Yalom, *A History of the Breast* (New York: Alfred A. Knopf, 1997).

p. 81. On female cadavers: Margaret Anne Doody, "Boom and Bust: Review of *A History of the Breast*, in *London Review of Books*, 19 June 1997, pp. 17–18.

p. 84. André Joly, "Toward a Theory of Gender in Modern English," in *Studies in English Grammer*, ed. by A. Joly and T. Fraser (Paris: Editions Universitaires, 1975), p. 271.

p. 84. Alfred Lubrano, " 'Canned Hunts' Become Target of Controversy," *Philadelphia Inquirer*, February 2, 1996, p. 1.

p. 85. Erik H. Erikson, *Gandhi's Truth: On the Origins of Militant Nonviolence* (New York: W. W. Norton & Co., 1969), p. 142.

p. 86. Philip Dray, *At the Hands of Persons Unknown: The Lynching of Black America* (New York: Random House, 2002), p. 81.

p. 87. "Man fucks woman; subject verb object," insight of Catharine MacKinnon in *Toward a Feminist Theory of the State*, p. 124.

p. 88. Duncan Murrell, "Bullwinkle's Death Ends Bowhunter's Quest," *Chapel Hill Herald*, September 19, 1996, p. 3

p. 88. "Quilty's," "Tables for Two," *The New Yorker*, December 7–14, 1990, p. 40.

p. 89. Martha Vicinus, "Sexuality and Power: A Review of Current Work in the History of Sexuality." *Feminist Studies* 8, no. 1 (Spring 1982): 133–56.

p. 90. "men can drive around . . ." in Høigård and Finstad, *Backstreets*, p. 89.

p. 91. Andrea Dworkin, *Pornography: Men Possessing Women* (New York: Perigee, 1981), pp. 25–26.

p. 92. Kimberlé Crenshaw, "Whose Story Is It, Anyway?: Feminist and Antiracist Appropriation of Anita Hill," in *Race-ing Justice, En-gendering Power*, edited by Toni Morrison (New York: Pantheon Books, 1992), p. 412.

p. 92. Jim Bouton, edited by Leonard Shecter, *Ball Four: Twentieth Anniversary Edition* (New York: Macmillan, 1970, 1990), p. 37

p. 92. "Burger chain franchise owner told to halt ammo ad." *The Dallas Morning News* (April 7, 1996), p. 7A.

p. 93. Joanna Bourke, *An Intimate History of Killing: Face-to-Face Killing in Twentieth-Century Warfare* (London: Granta Books, 1999), p. 254.

p. 98. Joan Dunayer, *Animal Equality* (Derwood, MD: Ryce Publishing, 2001), p. 69.

p. 100. Kathy Barry, *The Prostitution of Sexuality* (New York and London: New York University Press, 1995), pp. 35 and 34.

p. 100. Mimi Sheraton, "Love, Sex, and Flank Steak," *New Woman*, March 1996.

p. 103. MacKinnon, *Toward a Feminist Theory of the State*, p. 149.

p. 105. Andrea Lee, "The Emperor of Dreams," *The New Yorker*, July 28, 1997, p. 42.

p. 106. It is Sandra Bartky's insight that three disciplinary practices of appearance, gestures, and ornamentation exist.

p. 108. "The number of peepers," quoted in *Backstreets*, p. 88.

p. 113. Richard P. Kluft, M.D., "On the Apparent Invisibility of Incest: A Personal Reflection on Things Known and Forgotten," in *Incest-Related Syndromes of Adult Psychopathology*, ed. by Richard P. Kluft, M.D. (Washington, DC: American Psychiatric Press, Inc., 1990).

p. 114. Information on pigs from Temple Grandin, "Progress in Livestock Handling and Slaughter Techniques in the United States, 1970–2000" in *State of the Animals 2001*. At the Humane Society of the United States Web site http://www.hsus.org/ace/13167

p. 117. "Oink, oink, oink," "Pig-nics," "Pigorskia," and quotation from the lawyer are all from Bernard Lefkowitz, *Our Guys: The Glen Ridge Rape and the Secret Life of the Perfect Suburb* (Berkeley: University of California Press, 1997), pp. 128, 176, 383.

p. 118. Rape at Pi Eta off-campus Harvard Club, in Paul Langner, "Judge Imposes Gag Order in Rape Suit," *The Boston Globe*, November 13, 1990.

p. 118. Peggy Sanday, *Fraternity Gang Rape: Sex, Brotherhood, and Privilege on Campus* (New York and London: New York University Press, 1990), p. 11.

p. 118. Iris Chang, *The Rape of Nanking: The Forgotten Holocaust of World War II* (New York: Basic Books), 1997.

p. 123. Fromm quoted in Gerda Lerner, *The Creation of Patriarchy* (New York and Oxford: Oxford University Press, 1986), p. 199, Lerner's statement on p. 200.

p. 123. "bi-valved shellfish," Iris Furlong, "The Mythology of the Ancient Near East," in *The Feminist Companion to Mythology* (London: Pandora, 1992), p. 8.

p. 124. Diana York Blaine, "Necrophilia, Pedophilia, or Both? The Sexualized Rhetoric of the JonBenet Ramsey Murder," in *Sexual Rhetoric: Media Perspectives on Sexuality*,

Gender, and Identity, ed. M. Castarphen and S. Zavoina (Westport, CT: Greenwood Press, 1999), pp. 51–62.

p. 125. For a discussion of battering and harm to animals, see my article on that subject in eds. Carol J. Adams and Josephine Donovan, *Animals and Women: Feminist Theoretical Explorations* (Durham, NC: Duke University Press, 1996).

p. 128. Lorene Cary, *Black Ice* (New York: Vintage Books, 1991), p. 156.

p. 129. "Men act; women appear." See John Berger, *Ways of Seeing,* p. 47.

p. 130. Herbert Muschamp, "Beefcake for the Masses." *New York Times Magazine* (November 14, 1999), pp. 120–22.

p. 130. Anthony J. Cortese, *Provocateur: Images of Women and Minorities in Advertising* (Lanham, Boulder, New York, Oxford: Rowman and Littlefield, 1999).

p. 132. Suzanna Andrews, "She's Bare. He's Covered. Is There a Problem?" *New York Times* (November 1, 1992), pp. H13–14.

p. 135. Kelly Lynch quoted in "People in the News" in *Buffalo News,* November 12, 1991.

p. 135. Bobby Hull quoted in "Overheard," *Newsweek,* February 25, 1991, p. 13.

p. 135. Gael Greene quoted in "Perspectives," *Newsweek,* November 26, 2001, p. 21.

p. 136. Eric Schlosser, *Fast Food Nation: The Dark Side of the All-American Meal* (New York: Perennial, 2002), p. 197.

p. 137. John Berger, *Ways of Seeing.*

p. 138. on streetwalkers, *Backstreets,* p. 94.

p. 148. Jim Mason, "Inside a Turkey Factory," *Farm Sanctuary News* (Winter 1997), http://www.farmsanctuary.org/newsletter/newslet6.htm

p. 150. Joan Dunayer, "Sexist Words, Speciesist Roots," in *Animals and Women: Feminist Theoretical Explorations,* eds. Carol J. Adams and Josephine Donovan (Durham and London: Duke University Press, 1995), p. 13.

p. 151. Marilynn Marchione, "Ultrasound helps reveal cow falsies." *The Des Moines Register,* October 8, 2002.

p. 152. "Do you mind . . ." letter to Marilyn . . . plus answer, in *Parade* magazine, January 31, 1993, p. 10.

p. 155. Linda "Lovelace," (Linda Marchiano) with Mike McGrady, *Ordeal* (New York: Berkley Books, 1980), p. 113.

p. 155. MacKinnon on Marchiano, *Toward a Feminist Theory of the State.*

p. 160. Gloria Steinem, *Outrageous Acts and Everyday Rebellions* (New York: Holt, Rinehart and Winston, 1983), p. 180.

p. 161. Joan Dunayer, *Animal Equality,* p.160.

p. 163. "an image that oppresses . . ." in "No More Miss America! August 1968." In *Sisterhood Is Powerful,* ed. Robin Morgan (New York: Vintage Books, 1970), p. 521.

p. 163. Susan Douglas, *Where the Girls Are* (New York: Times Books, 1995), p. 159.

p. 163. Buss in Angier, *Woman: An Intimate Geography,* p. 357. For Angier's summary of evolutionary psychologists, see p. 356.

p. 164. Associated Press report on Kitten Reynolds, posted to the Web, July 9, 1999.

p. 166. On the Jacksonville Shipyards verdict, see "A Court Rules Well on Bias," editorial in *Buffalo News,* January 26, 1991, p. B-2.

p. 168. Ellyn Kaschak, *Engendered Lives,* p. 163.

p. 172. Maria Comninou, "Speech, Pornography, and Hunting," in *Animals and Women,* p. 133. My discussion on this page is deeply indebted to Comninou's article.

p. 172. Laura Lederer, "Introduction," in *The Price We Pay,* p. 7.

p. 173. Kaschak, *Engendered Lives,* p. 73.

DATE DUE

APR 16 2008			
DEC 1 3 2011			
APR 1 6 2014			